FIONA WIRRER-GEORGE OOCHUNYUNG, daughter of a Mbaiwum woman and an Austrian father, was raised by her grandparents and grew up between the two communities of Napranum (Weipa South) and Aurukun on the west coast of Cape York Peninsula. Fiona graduated from the National Aboriginal Islander Skills Development Association (Naisda) Dance College, Sydney, and James Cook University and has worked as a freelance performer and choreographer.

Her biography/family memoir about her grandmother Jean George, *Whispers of This Wik Woman*, won the 2003 David Unaipon Award and was published by UQP in 2004. It was also made into a play performed by the Kooemba Jdarra Theatre Company. She has written three other works for the stage and also written and published a children's book called *On Country: Stories of Nyrlotte* (2006). Fiona currently lives in Brisbane with her three daughters.

Double Native

FIONA WIRRER-GEORGE OOCHUNYUNG

UQP

First published 2012 by University of Queensland Press
PO Box 6042, St Lucia, Queensland 4067 Australia

www.uqp.com.au
uqp@uqp.uq.edu.au

Cataloguing-in-Publication Data is available from the
National Library of Australia
http://catalogue.nla.gov.au/

ISBN (pbk) 9 780 70223 917 5
ISBN (pdf) 9 780 70224 783 5
ISBN (epub) 9 780 70224 784 2
ISBN (kindle) 9 780 70224 785 9

Internal design by Sandy Cull, gogoGinko
Typeset in 12.5/17 pt Granjon by Post Pre-press Group, Brisbane
Printed in Australia by McPherson's Printing Group

University of Queensland Press uses papers that are natural, renewable and recyclable products made from wood grown in sustainable forests. The logging and manufacturing processes conform to the environmental regulations of the country of origin.

This book is dedicated to my lineage, past, present and future, especially Sheridan, Justice and Ebony, gems of my womb and the rainbow that colours my life.

part 1
Run With It

CHAPTER ONE

I'm running, running, running. I am aware of the shouting and the continuous cries of panic all around me, blanketing me, pushing and propelling me forward. I am aware of my mother's presence – the smell of her dress, her hair, the sound of her heart beating fast and wild in her chest. *Eracahm, eracahm, eracaahm!* The people chant rhythmically. *Orny oh, orny oh orny nan mun oooohhhhhhh!*

What? Where? I look around. People wrapped in flesh, blood and bone running. Where exactly are the ghosts? I think I see them. There are three. Two belong to our relatives: my granny's brother and old bada Sam Kerindun. I am told that they are angry that the people had summoned them back into the land of the living with song and dance, as is customary practice. My grandmother is in the front, leading the Wikway in song and dance – first *Sara* and then *Ghost Dance*. These spirits had been disturbed and had arrived among the people of the living with a strong energy. And now the people run!

I am aware of my heartbeat running a race of its own as I run too because, well, everyone else is doing it. They are all running, we are all running, but to where and why? What are the ghosts going to do if they do catch us? I just run. Lynette is on the other side of my mother and me.

'Run faster, Fay. Quick!'

We are rushed up the stairs and in the front door of a small timber house.

'Keep these little ones for me, Aunty,' Mum instructs the relative.

Then Mum's gone again along with the rest of the people. She has a baby firmly plonked on the side of her hip. I'm not sure which younger sister it is. The human stampede passes by, crying and wailing in unison. I peer outside cupping the sides of my face and pressing it up against the old dust-ridden plastic louvres, squinting in the hope that maybe I will get to see the spirits following them. Would I be able to recognise Grandfather Richard? I do remember what he looks like, I remind myself. Before he passed away in a car accident back in Weipa he would knock mangoes for me. His son, Granny Henry, also an uncle to me, was in the car with him along with my maternal grandfather. Daddy old man (that's what I used to call my grandad) and Granny Henry both survived the accident on the stretch of road just down from Six Tunnels, but Grandfather Richard didn't. Years later I'll understand that this ceremony that I am caught up in is performed to allow us to see our loved ones for the last time and to say goodbye once and for all. The families have decided to have a dual house opening for both men since both were leaders of the one nation. But for now I see nothing. Where are those spirits? I really want to see them.

'Sit down Fay otherwise them old fellas'll see you and try to take us,' instructs Lynette as she tugs at my dress.

I slide down the wall and bring both my knees up to my chest. I place my chin on my knees and turn my attention to the space I've been thrown into. The room is small and dark and warm and there's a glow in the corner as dim candlelight dances in slow motion. I try to slow down my breathing.

'*Merch ey*, granny girls? You two hungry?' questions the old lady who, for however long this takes, is now responsible for us. 'Damper there, look, and butter and jam.' She gestures toward the candlelit kitchen. There is a can of raspberry jam standing beside a can of butter. Both have been crudely cut open with the boomerang-shaped butcher's knife that now sits on top of the big-bellied damper. Several rust-ridden pannikins sit nearby waiting patiently to be filled with the strong black tea that sits steaming on the wooden stove. Tongues of fire rhythmically and lazily lick the inside of the dusty old stove as if they were a group of thirsty old lizards.

'No thank you,' I say.

I much preferred my own mother's cooking. I did not like eating at other people's houses, relative or not. Having said that, I did have one or two favourites whenever we were in Aurukun: *Cogai* Fred's place, which was more about free movies being at our disposal while we sat on the thick brown-and-yellow carpeted floor and *Pi* Violet's little old place where we sat around the fire waiting for geese and ashes damper or raided the huge outdoor pantry packed to the brim with biscuits, jam, cakes and flavoured cordial. *Pi* Violet was so giving, loving and gentle, always feeding us, always showing she cared. And, to our delight, meals around the campfire always ended with a story. My favourites were ghost stories. I always fought to be the lucky one who would snuggle on her lap. I'd stare up at the stars in the night sky and drift off to sleep with *Pi*'s soothing voice rocking my thoughts into the place where dreams came out to play.

'Well suit yourself, my granny girl, but this is going to be a long night by the looks a things,' the old granny had said that night, so many years ago now. She'd lit up an old tobacco pipe and puffed on it several times to get it smoking. I watched the smoke drift around the room, slowly caressing the darkness. Mine was a childhood of dancing with spirits – good, evil and mysterious. A childhood in which there was a fine line between this world and the afterlife or the world of spirits. A childhood where not only Nan, but all who were qualified communicated with the spirits quite naturally and regularly. Us kids were constantly warned not to overstep the boundaries that only just separated the two realms.

Earlier that day the house of Grandfather Richard had been opened with ceremony for the first time in over a year. I can still smell the muskiness. I clearly remember being sardined in among the other mourners, as wailing and protestations of his passing and his absence left the lips of many a local. The closure of his house when he died forbade any sort of human presence or activity to take place until the appropriate ceremonial practice unlocked it. Only then could the house be lived in again. Only then would his spirit be released back to his country. Until his house was opened the adults were constantly warning us: 'Youse'll get sick if you touch something you not supposed to. Menfolk who have been through business will *otapee* you and your belly will get big and swollen and then you will have to look for someone to rub you and put smell on you. That will be a nuisance.' It was common knowledge and understanding that beyond the safety of our own home and away from the watchful eyes of our closest, most trusting relatives danger was everywhere, particularly involving the spiritual realm.

'Play very carefully,' Nan'd say. 'Spirits are everywhere. Secret business is everywhere. You need to know which parts of the land you must not overstep.'

I felt that I would be alright. I had a very wise and knowledgeable grandmother who feared almost nothing. She did, however, fear the living God, the God of the Bible. That was something I knew from a very early age. She was also extremely protective, to the point of smothering me, but, luckily, she was not as fast as me. I could run and indeed I did. If I needed to get away from the prying eyes of my seniors all I had to do was instruct my legs.

I was born Maryann Fiona George just after midnight on 2 January 1969 at the old General Hospital on Thursday Island. I was actually due on New Year's Day but I chose to be late. If I had been born on New Year's Day I reckon people would remember my birthday more often. As it is, they're too busy recovering from New Year's Eve celebrations, so it's quite a lonely day for me. I've been told that the doctor who delivered me had wanted to cut the birthmark off my neck shortly after I was born. It's known as a strawberry, but back then it probably looked more like the saggy piece of skin under a chicken's neck. My mother refused to let him operate as she feared that I would not survive the procedure. It's still on the left side of my neck, but has reduced in size.

It wasn't until I was in my late twenties that I noticed nothing had been inserted in the father's section on my birth certificate. I was curious about this. I didn't like the fact that there was no name, it disturbed me. It made me feel like I had just fallen out of the sky or something.

I was one of those children you see running around an Aboriginal community and immediately a question would surface. Why is that girl fair skinned? Who is her father? Which mob does she belong to? I had a mother, a granny, a daddy old man (my grandfather), an uncle who was married to my mother and was the father of my younger sisters, an older sister who also wasn't the biological daughter of this uncle, many cousins, other uncles and aunties, and lots of other grannies as well. A big family! But there was no dad. Well, no dad who was my real dad, the man who made me. I often wondered how I came to be. I would look at my skin – I was shades lighter in comparison to most of the other kids. More orange or golden, I thought. A bit like the colour of syrup. Yummy syrup. I liked syrup on hot damper with half-melted butter. I'd cut roads into my damper so the butter and syrup would mix together and sink deep into the cake.

And my hair – curly and golden bronze, not dark and spirally like my family members' and relatives'. But this was my family. Of course I belonged here.

The old pre-school was in Peppan Street in my home community of Napranum. *Thy* Joyce Charger was not only the director but also the head teacher. I have only vague memories of her book reading and instructive voice, but do remember lining up on the veranda of a building that stood where the old basketball courts once were. At the back of this building was a big pond that was dry for most of the year. During the wet season we'd scoop tadpoles from this pond.

At home, Grandfather would sit beside the smoking fire with one leg up and the other bent underneath him as he stripped back the flesh of goanna or snake and fed it into my mouth. He'd give me a questioning look; I'd either nod in appreciation or ask permission to spit the food back out. Both goanna and snake are oily, tough, quite bland and stringy in taste and texture. Even as a small child I was taught how to locate the lolly part inside mud crab or fish eggs. The marrow of ibis or jabiru was another delicacy I came to appreciate very early on. We were taught how to peel back the outer skin of the flying fox to extract the meat. Each of us would be given up to five or six of these bats on a piece of paperbark and, as with the jabiru, we'd crack open the bone and suck out the marrow. Some meals, anywhere between five and ten turtle eggs would be boiled then poured over hot rice or damper – these were treats us kids would always look forward to. Piniwinkles *ndrangle*, long bum *pri*, accool *chaay*, witchety grubs *argorich* – and the list goes on – are the foods my sisters and I were brought up on. Well, maybe not *argorich*. I could not bring myself to even contemplate eating this. No amount of probing would convince me to consume this grub.

I have strong memories of my great-grandmother's country Wathaniin – panja, the smell and taste of warm homemade bread, the waterlilies and swamps and especially the legend of *kootheeth erdin*, which refers to small ghosts or fairies. I remember playing lots of bush games. Firm, straight tree branches would be cut to the right length to serve as a bat, and we'd hit seed pods big enough to serve as balls in an improvised game of vigoro on the little grassy, uneven airstrip. Mum had taught us this game. She said she'd played it as a kid when she lived in the mission dormitory back in Weipa during the late forties and early fifties.

I recall running through the big old house on our arrival at Wathaniin in the late seventies. I immediately fell in love with the place. Who would've thought you'd find a huge Queenslander house in the middle of isolated Wik country? The kitchen was spacious, warm and inviting. A huge home-baked, round-bellied bread would sit invitingly on the big old table in the centre of the room – the smell is still fresh in my memory. I'd cut my share as thick as and dress it with butter and spread. Looking out the window at the bushland that wrapped itself around this lone, man-made structure I could smell the swamp nearby. One day Aunty promised us kids a walk there to collect lilies.

'But!' she warned. 'We must be careful of the fairies!'

My eyes had widened with excitement. Fairies! Just like the ones in the storybooks back in my school library at Weipa. Wow!

'Which fairies, Aunty? Where they? What they look like? Can we make friends with them? Can I talk to them? Are they families to us?'

'Settle down, girl. We'll see if they'll pay us a visit. Just be careful though, they like to take things.'

'Like what?'

'Well, like your thongs maybe, or your clothes if we decide to go swimming.'

'Are they dangerous? Will or can they hurt us?'

'I don't think so, girl. But they are mischievous, we know

that for sure. Stories have been passed down to us from the old people who have seen these fairies. We have to be careful. We might get old fella to put smell on us first to protect us. Can't be too sure, you know.'

Receiving the smell off males offers us protection from illness that may be caused supernaturally.

I made a note to confirm everything Aunty had told us about the fairies that day with Nan and to seek out any additional information that would be valuable.

Nyrlotte! Rare-white waterlily, my sissy's name, my great-grandmother's name. Nyrlotte, Wathaniin, Ornyawa.

I can clearly recall lying on Granny Christina Chevathen's lap one day in Aurukun. She was brushing my hair.

'Snake is *thook*. Now you say it,' she instructed.

'*Thook*,' I repeated.

'Good girl! And wallaby is *punk*. Now you try.'

'*Punk*,' I said laughing. 'Just like a punk rocker, hey? Wallaby with pink and purple fur.'

'Yes,' she said, as my sisters, cousins and I all broke out into fits of laughter.

She continued naming all the reptiles, bush animals, sea life and birds of the air. We were learning culture. '*Pikuw* is crocodile, *mye* is tucker, *menth* is nice, *chaprah* is blood.' She went on and on. 'Next I'll teach you some sentences and then we can talk to each other in *munkan*, granny girl, okay?'

'Tell me some rude words, Granny,' I commanded.

'No, you don't want to know rude words, bubba.'

'Yes I do, tell me pleeeease.'

'Okay,' she responded giving in easily to my pleading. 'But you must not use them. I'm only telling you so you know if someone else uses these words around you and you will know what they are saying, okay?'

I nodded excitedly and the others all sat up in eager expectation.

'Now don't tell Mummy or Granny I'm teaching you these swear words, okay. It's our secret?'

'Yep,' I nodded.

She lowered her voice and began to fill our young minds.

CHAPTER TWO

Even after I started primary school, for some reason or another I made regular visits to the newly built pre-school. I recall click-clocking around in oversized high heels, playing dress-up in grown-up clothes and nursing my little brown doll, feeding it, giving it its bottle. I made numerous phone calls to make-believe people on the old black telephone that stood in the corner of the play section. Outside in the sandpit I formed shapes and built sandcastles with the coloured plastic moulds and little bucket and spade. I can still remember the cool wetness of the sand. I recall too the smell of butcher's paper as I smacked on all the colours of the rainbow, aimlessly creating a pattern while the paint dripped back onto my arms and hands, down to the bottom of the easel and onto the ground.

In Years 1 and 2, we'd sit on the floor to go through our alphabet. Hand puppets helped with our phonics. My personal puppet was the green frog one, although I did have competition from another student whose name also started with the letter F.

One afternoon after school, I had been wandering around the grounds when I heard voices coming from my classroom. Peeping through the louvres I could see my teacher and another male teacher. They appeared to be wrestling each other, nudging their way through each other's clothing. Miss was struggling to position herself on our art table, all the while making grunting and gasping noises as if she couldn't breathe or was drowning and needed rescuing. Sir appeared to be getting more and more excited by the sounds his colleague was making. So this must be what teachers get up to in the classroom after school, I thought to myself.

One time in Year 2, we had to decorate an egg carton like a caterpillar, an activity following the reading of the storybook *The Very Hungry Caterpillar*, one of my favourite books at school. After the session we were directed to place our completed creations on the bench and collect them at going-home time. When school finished, I searched everywhere for my caterpillar. Some other kids told me that another girl had it and was hooking it home. I spotted her at the school gates.

'Hey, Samantha, you got my caterpillar, bring it back here,' I called out.

'Nah, this mine,' she called back.

'Nah, that's mine, you ask Miss. I made that one, bring it back here.'

'You wanna fight, ay?'

'I fight you under the almond tree.'

The cheek of her. Firstly taking my caterpillar and claiming it was hers and then, if that wasn't enough, suggesting I fight for it on turf I considered to be ours. That almond tree was my tree; Nan planted that tree.

'I'll fight you alright.'

And fight it out we did.

Early on into my schooling I realised I loved books. I hung out in the library quite frequently as there weren't really any books at home, apart from the odd *Archie* comic or *Reader's Digest* magazines that Mum had accumulated over the years. I loved the Dick Roughsey and Percy Trezise collections, including *The Giant Devil Dingo* as well as most of the fairytales. I knew I wanted to tell stories and write books from around Year 4 onwards when I realised that the books available to me did not depict the world and people that were familiar to me.

Even though I was a hard worker in class, I wasn't always the most obedient. There was a time when I decided not to go back to class after the bell had gone off at morning tea. I had been enjoying my time way up high in the large mango tree.

'Let's just keep playing, you mob,' I ordered the other kids. 'Who's in?'

The tiggy game across the mango tree continued on for the remainder of the day.

'Whose idea was this?'

Mr Star, our principal, had tracked us down and marched us all back to his office halfway through our final tiggy session for the day. He and another teacher had stood standing at the bottom of the tree for a good ten or fifteen minutes as I contemplated whether we should oblige and 'climb down this instant'.

Eventually I succumbed to the pressure and, consequently, so did the others.

'It was her idea, Sir,' dobbed the annoying boy who would not stop staring at me in class every day.

He really did give me the creeps. I shot him the meanest look I could conjure up.

'What? No.' I lied. 'It wasn't me.'

'No point in lying, young Miss. It makes sense that this would be your idea. You're always telling the others what to do.'

Mr Star was a tall, well-built white man with a moustache. He was always either growling at me or ridiculing me in front of the class. He often kept me in at morning tea and lunch times as well. He reckoned that I was too cheeky with my backchatting. Come to think of it, I don't think he liked me at all. He appeared to always enjoy challenging me.

'Now, what do you think I should do with you lot?'

He was looking straight at me even though there were six or seven of us in his office.

'Send us back to class, Sir,' was my response.

'What, just like that, without any punishment? Don't you think that the cane would be more appropriate, young Miss?'

'Nah,' I shook my head.

'Why not?'

'Because we girls.'

'Because you're girls?' he laughed almost mockingly. 'Regardless of that fact, you and your loyal followers still knowingly broke the school rules, so there must be punishment.'

'Punish us in a different way then, Sir. Just don't cane us.'

'And how, young Miss?'

'I don't know, Sir, you decide. Just no cane, that's all.'

Mr Star stared at me long and hard before continuing.

'And what should I do with the boys then?'

'Oh, you can cane them, but you really should let us girls go.'

Mr Star looked at me with a confused, but also slightly amused, look on his face.

'Very well,' he said to us girls, 'get back to class quick smart. I shall think of another form of punishment in due course.'

The boys had to remain behind. They got a strap each across the knuckles. I wasn't very popular among the boys for quite some time after that.

Another time we were all lined up at parade under the covered area. I was in Year 5 and our teacher was Mr Longfoot. We were sitting listening to whoever was up the front when I happened to look sideways. Mr Longfoot was crouching with one leg up slightly higher than the other with his testicles hanging out the side of his pants. Couldn't he feel it? Was he not uncomfortable? Clearly not. There he was, styling up thinking he was deadly while keeping an eye on his class with this mental-looking smile on his face. I nudged the girl beside me and pointed in Mr Longfoot's direction. We both snuck a little laugh together as I indicated for her to bring his goods to the attention of the girl beside her and the next girl and the next girl. Soon the entire row was transfixed by the spectacle.

Wandering around our community after school, us kids would often venture off into forbidden territory. We'd explore Lake Patricia, Lake McLeod, then we'd track on to Six Tunnels and onto Blue Water, which was near the airport. As if this wasn't enough, I would often try to get the others to continue on to Cool Pool. This swimming hole was a beautiful, secluded paradise tucked away deep in the bush and away from town and the community. Vehicle-wise, the only way to it was by four-wheel drive although occasionally smaller cars would brave the narrow winding dirt roads riddled with potholes. The main lagoon at Cool Pool snaked deeper into dense bush country and so remained basically untouched by humans. Swamp reeds surrounded the swimming area; the water was cool, dark and deep. I often wondered about crocodiles, and would sometimes swear they were about, but then the desire to become one with the water would overcome me and hungry reptiles sporting sharp teeth would be the last thing on my mind.

'You mob be careful, *cambahl* around somewhere,' the adults would warn us.

Regardless of the possible threat of crocodiles we collectively loved this part of country. Besides, this area was popular for *thooth* string or swamp grass. We needed *thooth* string to make dilly bags and grass skirts required for ceremony. We were always told that as long as there was noise and constant commotion the crocs would not strike, that it would be too confusing for them to do so.

A huge tree right on the bank accommodated a large rope that someone had taken it upon themselves to string up. It never failed to keep us kids occupied with constant swing-dives into the lagoon over and over again. I absolutely loved this place and always felt a special connection to it. Much later on, as an adult, this connection would be confirmed and explained to me. But even as a kid I always felt that Cool Pool was, for some reason or another, *my place*.

At celebration and ceremony time in Aurukun there'd be a lot of dancing going on. We'd make the trip from Weipa to be with family and participate in the ceremonial process as required. People would be filling their plates to the brim, eating to their heart's content. Prepared in the earth oven was a feast of pig, wallaby, geese, brolga, flying fox and sea turtle. Earth-oven baked damper, potato, kumara, pumpkin and onion, curry beef stew, rice, iced cakes sprinkled with hundreds and thousands, biscuits, red and green cordial and salads were laid out on tables. Streamers, balloons and coconut palms decorated the performance area marked out with white sand, a practice learnt from the Torres Strait Islanders when Aboriginal men from the Cape spent time in the Strait during World War II.

I love the dancing. I'm sitting *babuk*, or cross-legged, right up the front. There's been a lot of *thaipu* already. Grandad's *Captain Banks* and *Apo regeh* have been danced and sung. *Cogai* Fred's *Yenji Yenji* has been danced over and over until the men pant and sweat profusely, drenching their white singlets and the red calico wrapped around their waists. On their arms and ankles are strips of white material or *muk muk*. There is powdering and perfume spraying and offerings of money to the most entertaining or favoured of dancers, also according to Island custom.

Enough of this *thaipu*, I think to myself. I prefer the cultural dances, the real tribal ones. Just my luck – a proper traditional one is about to begin. I quickly realise that I don't like the masks the dancers have on. The masks personify the devil. They look powerfully confronting and send a shiver through me. The singing and action begins. The dancers move forward in a stamping action as the balls of their feet press into the sand, causing a mini dust-storm. Their heads move in a stoical manner from side to side as each dancer focuses straight ahead. The sound of the singing is both mystifying and intriguing. And even though it's disturbing, I am drawn to this dance. It affects my belly, my inside, in a deep and stirring way. One of the dancers is looking straight at me. He continues to stamp and move his head from side to side, all the time closing in on the distance between him and me. I look straight back at him. I can see his eyes in the dim lighting. Why is he taking all this time to just look at me? I look around. Nobody else appears to be aware of him.

Now he's freaking me out a little. I pull both my feet up and cup the outside of my knees in response to the chill I'm experiencing. I don't even recognise this dancer. Usually you can by knowing someone's height or hair or figure, but he is someone I don't know. I don't even recognise the dance, even though I usually know which group the dances belong to. Is this a dream?

My memories of living in Aurukun are indeed sweet. Even though Weipa was my main home community a large portion of my childhood was spent in Aurukun – on trips taken during school holidays or at ceremony. Ceremonial periods would usually last weeks, often months at a time. Back then life consisted mainly of play, family business and cultural activities. And eating, lots of eating. Food was never readily available though. Apart from ceremonial or festival time, the cupboard only ever held the bare essentials: plain flour, baking powder, tea leaf, powdered milk, syrup or jam and white sugar. Occasionally, a bag of potatoes and some onions would make a delightful addition to the catch of the day. It was not about the fridge, the pantry, the take-away or the shops. It was always about looking for food. When you needed food you had to go search or hunt (depending very much on the season): digging the earth, climbing the trees, peering in the shrubbery, scanning the waters, trudging through the mangroves, sifting through the mud and the sand and then preparing and finally consuming. Survival was all about your skill: how well you saw; how far you could walk; how fast you could run; how careful and quiet you could be in the water; how far up in the tree you could climb; how far down into the earth you could dig; how long you could sit on the beach with your line out or with your spear in hand; how accurately you could spear that fish, or stingray or crab, and then – a further challenge – not let it get away.

The time I spent at Ambracan Kakalkan in the seventies makes up some of my best childhood memories. Trudging through the swamp at Yagalmunkun, Wuthan or at Wathaniin, clearing the area of swamp grass, and then plonking myself comfortably on the earth to dig for *panja*. I ache when I realise that my own daughters, particularly my youngest, will most probably never get to experience any of this. Grannies, aunties, sisters and mothers would be all over the swampy area, busy with the tedious but enjoyable task of collecting the mud-coated swamp nut. Uncles, fathers, grandfathers and brothers would continue further on in search of brolga, ibis or geese. Wild pigs, wallaby or jabiru also added to the day's catch. On their return to camp, an earth oven would be prepared using gathered stones, leaves and paperbark. Wild honey, *panja*, lily stalks, damper, various bush fruits and nuts would satisfy our hungry bellies in the meantime.

I recall the taste of *panja*, sweet but sour. I absolutely love the smell of *eginthaķ*, or sugar bag as it is commonly known. I loved looking for *eginthak*, too. Scooping the bush honey and the honeycomb out and proudly presenting it on paperbark back at camp was always a highlight during our times out bush.

I am eleven years old and although I live the majority of the time with Nan I am at Mum's whenever it's convenient. This day I leave Mum's and make my way across the sports oval toward Nan's house. I stare down at my feet, noticing how they blend in with the dry grass and earth. I notice how they mould in with the land. I love how my feet feel when I am walking the land, running the land – the feel of the sand, water, grass, rocks, pebbles, trees, leaves – dodging the sharp stones, bindi-eye and even the broken bottle glass that often invades my path.

This day I can feel and sense someone. This person is inside of me, somewhere. She is not like the family I know to be my family, not at all. She is dressed differently and she looks different. Very different. But I feel I know her. I don't know how or why. She is a white woman, but not like the white women who are our teachers or nurses who live in the community. She is not even like the white women I see in the magazines or catalogues. She's different still. She's a woman from somewhere else, from a land far away, perhaps across the seas somewhere. White in skin colour, but her eyes are of culture and so is the spirit that peers out from behind them. She reminds me of the women in movies I've seen on television; a hard-working, wise, stern woman. On her head she wears a scarf and she's dressed mainly in black.

I snap back to reality. Only a couple of seconds have passed, but it feels as if time has stood still. This woman knows me, that is the reason why she watches over me. She is looking straight at me, straight into my eyes.

I look to my right then to my left. No cars, so I quickly sprint across the road to Nan's place.

One afternoon, I had just exited the school grounds following a full-on day of athletics. I was exhausted. I had been running my heart out for my team *Twal*, which means eagle in the local dialect. Our opposing house team was *Baidum*, a Torres Strait Islander word for shark. It was after three o'clock and the schoolyard and surrounding area was filled with commotion. I'm not sure how I got into an argument with a fellow student – a sight for sore eyes, I might add. This particular boy was not a nice person. In fact, I don't think he was ever nice to anyone. He had always made me feel uneasy. Every time I heard him talk he seemed to be verbally attacking someone – insulting or threatening them.

We were just at the school gates when he said it.

'You're a bastard you know? A yellow bastard.'

I stopped for a moment. What exactly was a yellow bastard? I looked back at this scrawny, unpleasant-looking boy. He eyeballed me and shot the words toward me once more, just to make sure I'd heard him clear and proper.

'You're a bastard!'

I didn't know what to say. I honestly did not know what it meant. But, of course, I had to say something back to him. I had studied my grandmother enough to know that you don't just back down, not in any situation.

'You now, you're the bastard,' I fired back at him.

He laughed. 'Sorry, you're the bastard. You're the one without a father. I got a dad, I know who my father is.'

That moment would forever change everything for me. My entire outlook, my responses, my thoughts, the way I felt not only about myself but each of my family members and my place in my extended family was never the same from that moment on.

'Mama, what does bastard mean?' I asked when I got home. 'No,' I paused. 'What does yellow bastard mean?'

Mum looked at me, puzzled.

'What you asking me that for? Did someone say something to you?'

I nodded.

'Who?'

I gave the name of the boy.

'That trouble-making, useless, good-for-nothing boy. Don't take notice of him. What's he good for? He's a good-for-nothing ugly little thing, he is!'

'Yeah, but why did he call me that? Is that what I am? Am I a yellow bastard? What's a bastard anyway? And I'm not yellow, I'm brown, and I don't think there's anything wrong with it. It's different but there's nothing wrong with it.'

'Goodness me, girl, just leave it alone. You are not a bastard, you have a dad.'

'Well where is he? Who is he? How come I don't ever see him?'

'His name is Fred Wirrer. He is your father.'

'But where is he?'

'He just left one day when you were little.'

CHAPTER THREE

Camping at Bung was simply the best – a beautiful, untouched part of country. Almost every holiday us kids would find ourselves unloading the hired dinghy with our swag and requirements for the two-week – sometimes the entire six-week – Christmas break. We'd all fight for either our own little tent or mosquito net to keep the mossies as well as the cool sting of the night and early morning dew off us. We'd erect our own coverings right there on the water's edge and that would be home for the duration of the camp (I know, where were the crocs?). About a hundred metres further inland a large tarpaulin would be erected to serve as the main cooking and storage area. Frequent trips over to Evans Landing on the north side would be made in order to purchase perishables, treats and ice, if we were fortunate enough to have an esky.

Night after night we'd fall asleep under the deepest darkest sky blanketed with millions of stars while listening to Nan's soothing voice as she yarned stories of her childhood. Fish would playfully dance in front of us, the fire spreading its warm glow, the sound of the waves gently lulling our spirits into slumber.

Directly behind our campsite, a couple of hundred metres further in toward the bush, stood a huge fig tree. It was massive! I loved this tree; it was my favourite hangout and hiding spot. I'd scramble up the thick stump and balance my foot like a trapeze artist along one of the huge branches that stretched out as if it were a long arm pointing to something out at sea. On reaching the outer section, I'd comfortably position myself in a spot where I could balance for hours on end. While there I'd munch on wild bush fruits like bumbums, wongais and beernuts, which I'd have gathered before my ascent to this secret hiding place. I had a full view of the open sea as well as of the comings and goings of family. I was also in hearing distance if any family member required my assistance during the day.

One day as I was trudging through the bush looking for bushfruits, a large goanna began chasing me. There I was being chased by the goanna, followed by my dog Stubby, all of us running in the one direction. After a pretty dramatic climb up a small tree – in fear of my life – it seemed like a lifetime later, that I stumbled back to camp with Stubby proudly trotting beside me, a bloody and limp dead reptile hanging from his mouth. On reaching camp I watched as my grandfather proudly accepted the goanna and immediately began to prepare it for consumption. Straight into the hot ashes it went. Goanna for afternoon tea!

On these trips, Nan would take me aside and point out the story places and their cultural and traditional significance. This knowledge will remain inside of me until such time as it is necessary to share it.

Another part of country frequented by my family during the holidays was Beening Creek. A regular chore was to accompany my mother at dawn to collect firewood. As we left camp and continued on I would watch the sun slowly peer out from behind the trees. I remember listening to the chorus of birds taking flight overhead or in the branches all around us, the sweet early morning smell in the air, the sound of splashes from the nearby creek – were they crocodiles or barramundi? Although we were taught of the dangers of *cambahl* we also accepted that they were part of our country. We just had to exercise caution, wisdom and common sense when near their turf. I loved these early morning duties. Mum'd often suggest we make a detour and collect rosella on the way back. I would immediately begin to search the shrubs as that meant we'd have jam later that day to spread on damper or scones.

During our spare time I enjoyed time spent swimming in the ponds. One main one, where we all went swimming, appeared to be the safest of the cluster. At the one next to it the reeds seemed to grow a lot thicker and higher. I always suspected there were crocodiles in that one. Why wouldn't there be? They lived in the creek a couple of hundred metres away, so of course they would make their way into the pond. Separated by a small hill was a series of smaller, more deserted ponds that, from time to time, I'd visit by myself, much to the ignorance of my elders. I'm pretty sure we were warned never to wander to these ponds, for both obvious and unknown reasons, but I always took Stubby with me for company and as a safeguard. We knew that this was not only our home; it also belonged to *cambahl* as well.

On one lone walk I stumbled upon a man who appeared to be doing something that I thought was peculiar. He was someone I didn't know and it looked like he was urinating. I can't remember if he had his trousers on or if they were down around his feet but both hands seemed to be in front of his middle section, as if cupping something, and his head was facing downwards. I didn't have time to take in what was happening as he must've heard me and immediately swung around. I made eye contact with him, which was a bad thing, before turning and bolting. Running back to camp I recalled one of Nan's many warnings: 'Never ever look into the eyes of a man you don't know, especially when we out bush.'

By the afternoon word had gotten around the camp about my encounter with the stranger, which resulted in me getting a flogging.

'Fiona, you realise what could happen to you now. Huh?' Nan admonished.

I shook my head nervously, trying my best to refrain from crying.

'If that man was doing business you could get sick. Did you see his face? Do you know who it was?'

'I saw him, but I don't know him.'

'Did he see you?'

I shook my head.

'Yes he did,' I answered.

'Oh goodness gracious me, he must be traveller, someone from somewhere else. But what was he doing here? Old-fella must stay up all night until dawn just in case that fella come snooping around here.'

Daddy old man acknowledged this with a silent nod.

'And you, you *arndraht* little wanderer, you wander away again by yourself and you'll be copping more than a flogging, you hear?'

I knew better than to muck around with Nan. If I was ever tempted to disobey her all I'd have to do was look at the scar above my left breast. This went back to one afternoon when Nan was sitting contentedly on the beach at a place known commonly as Fish Trap. Lyn and I were with her. We kept ourselves amused by skidding that brown pod known to us as *nthepal*, or *ḵulap* to the Torres Strait Islanders, along the water's edge. We'd skid the pods across the surface then dive in after them. Nan calmly kept asking us not to swim near her line as we'd disturb any fish nearby. But Lyn and I continued on, disobeying her, not intentionally, just because we were enjoying ourselves so much. All of a sudden I felt a stinging sensation on my chest. When I surfaced for air I noticed that I had been cut on the left of my chest, exposing the flesh. The salt water made the pain worse. It appeared that I had landed on an oyster bed, and so suffered the consequences of not obeying Nan. I immediately ran over to her.

'*Yaḵay*, *yaḵay*, Nan look ya what be happen.'

I was crying and expected her to be sympathetic. Instead she grabbed a thin stick and proceeded to whack me with it until she was satisfied.

'Don't come to me. I don't want you. Did you listen to me? Hey? Go, go to your mother and cry. You not getting any sympathy from me, you disobedient careless child.'

I had to get out of there quick smart. But I got only as far as the school grounds when it began to pour down rain. A storm had been brewing all that afternoon and finally hit. I ran under cover and hid in one of the corners of the building, all the while crying my eyes out, feeling devastatingly alone.

Some of our camping trips were to Mangrove Island, or Mbouchat as it is traditionally known, an hour's trip by road heading north. I absolutely loved going to Mbouchat. Apart from daily trips gathering bush foods, the highlight was swimming in the creek that separated the two banks we camped on. An old tree, which had fallen across the creek, made a bridge so us kids could cross back and forth at our convenience. I especially loved swimming at night. We would dive into the water with a torch in one hand and a small spear in the other in search of catfish. Under the old tree logs we'd go exploring, as well as delving under the embankments. We believed a short devil man lived in these crevices and would come out at night and wander through the camp. Over the years a handful of kids claimed to have experienced personal encounters with this devil man. They would often wake up either beside the bank or on the sand away from the rest of us. Who's to know whether it was just sleepwalking or not? But when you get a white girl, the daughter of the community manager, experiencing the same things then you have to take notice. It was common and normal for us black kids to have encounters with spirits and ghosts but when Kerri started waking up by the edge of the riverbank and claimed that she too had seen a 'devil man' throughout the night then it took the whole ordeal to another level.

Sometimes we'd go to Wooldrun Creek.

'Hey you mob, look what I found,' my cousin said on one trip out there.

She was on watch outside as four of us rummaged through a makeshift timber hut that had been illegally erected near the bank. What a haul! Cans of braised steak and onion, corned beef, spaghetti and meatballs and a selection of vegetables including corn, peas and carrots were stacked to the brim on the upper shelf. Anzac, Iced VoVo and Scotch Finger biscuits took up most of the second shelf along with matches, kerosene, lanterns, toilet paper, UHT milk, white sugar, raspberry jam and treacle. I noticed the corner pages of several magazines sticking out from under a pillow. A quick flick of their contents revealed an assortment of naked white girls in various exposing positions. My initial reaction was shock, then numbness then curiosity. Oh my God! I couldn't let my sisters and cousins see these pictures. After some thought I informed the gang that we should make a fire on the bank as I had found some rude magazines and thought we should burn them.

'You can't do that, Fay.'

'Why not? They're rude.'

'But they're not ours to burn, and anyway if we do that then them whitefellas'll know someone's been in their hut and they'll straightaway know it was us. We the only mob camping just up the beach a bit.'

'So, we'll just say it wasn't us, plenty people pass by this way in their boats or stop and fish. We'll say it could be anyone. Besides, they didn't ask if they could build these huts. This not their land, this our place!'

'Nah, Fay, why don't we tell Mum and them? They'll know what to do.'

'No, Nan gonna flog us for coming in the hut in the first place, and she'll flog me for just seeing these pictures. Let's just burn 'em, it'll teach these men a lesson.'

'It's not our place to teach 'em. You forgetting, Fay? We the kids, they're the grown-ups. They can read this sort a magazine if they want to. They can do whatever they want.'

'Well then they should be careful. They shouldn't be able to do what they like. They disrespecting our land with their rubbish, I reckon.'

The debate continued on and off for the next hour or so as we swam in the creek and helped ourselves to the biscuits. In the end I decided to put the magazines back where I had found them and made the others promise not to look at them, not even a peek.

'If you do,' I warned them, 'what you see will burn your eyes. You'll see them white girls sitting down proper wrong way with nothing on and you'll see their, you know . . . their private place . . . full on!'

'What! They don't even have pants on?'

'Proper nothing!'

Everyone's eyes and mouths widened in shock, but I'm sure the male cousins were curious. Whether the others heeded this order of mine or not I don't know. They had many opportunities to sneak back to the hut. In fact, no matter where we were on country, whether camping or just out for the day, I would come across these types of magazines as well as XXXX cans, cask packets, cigarette butts, soft-drink cans and chip packets. Our land had clearly become a dumping ground.

Sometime in my early secondary school years we moved up to Callope Street. All us kids in the street would invite each other to our birthday parties. Aunty Peah Woosup would go all out and make the biggest feast and let the entire street turn up. She'd have pots of chicken cooked in various ways, rice, *amay* damper, fried scones and *kup moari* pig, turtle and dugong. The tables would be groaning with sweets, cakes, biscuits, custard, canned fruit and watermelon. There'd be so much food left over that it would last for days.

I especially loved it when it was my birthday. Mum always made an effort to celebrate our birthdays regardless of the lack of money in the household. She made everything from scratch. Us kids would have to go and raid the lemon trees near where the whitefellas lived for her to make ice-cold lemonade. She'd bake patty cakes and the birthday cake – chocolate or vanilla – would always have either bright blue, pink or yellow icing. Sometimes she'd make orange-flavoured homemade cake and we'd get to choose the colour for the topping. But my favourite was blue icing on chocolate cake.

CHAPTER FOUR

I'm on the starting line and the sound of the gunshot is only a fraction of a second away even though the wait feels like an eternity. The teacher is standing on the sideline with his arm extended straight up into the air, his finger on the trigger. At any given second he's going to press down on it. The initial challenge here is to not start too early nor too late. My heart is beating overtime – I'm aware of it dancing in my chest. My palms are sweaty and all I want is to get going. This adrenalin rush is going to blind all my senses for the next ten seconds or so.

I'd been running for a while by this stage, and loving every second of it. With the 100, 200, 400 and even 800-metre races it was as if my body went on autopilot and did what it needed to do to win. Running excited me all through my primary school years and into high school. I thrived on the lead-up to, as well as the actual competing in, sport and athletic carnivals. Winning became my main focus and the discipline that was required to heighten my chances of coming first was good for me. I didn't always win, of course, but year after year the medals and the trophies were mostly headed in my direction. There were maybe two other girls who could top me in the shorter sprints. One of them, like me, was able to intellectually calculate what was required to win over both the short and long distances and command the body to make the necessary adjustments and deliver. This girl was my competition, and was probably just that fraction better than me even in primary school. The 1500 metres and the cross-country races required endurance and with these I had time to think, calculate my approach, be aware of what needed adjusting and so forth. In the 1500 metres my strategy was to always get in front immediately, then sit on a steady pace that would keep me in front, finishing with a sprint in the last 60 metres or so.

I especially enjoyed those last few moments of a race; I found it extremely exhilarating. Tearing down that lane with your school team, family members and friends cheering you on. All eyes are on you, they appear to be breathing in unison with you, they witness every movement you make, it appears to be happening in slow motion, they're on that journey with you every step of the way until you cross that line. And when you do, they embrace the air and the moment with shouts and physical expressions of joy because of you, with you and for you. I absolutely loved it.

'It's not fair,' sooked a tall white girl one day during morning tea.

I had been sitting under the black wattle tree listening to the crows competing for the breadcrumbs that blanketed the area around me. This girl was a good runner by the school's standards and was always seen practising out on the oval with the Physical Education teacher during her lunch period or after school.

'Hey?' I turned to her. 'What's not fair?' I continued, amid mouthfuls of a Vegemite roll creatively sandwiched with barbeque chips.

'You guys!'

'What you mean, you guys? Who and what you talking 'bout?'

'I train every day and yet you guys just turn up on sports day and win. It's not fair. How come youse are all just so good? And you don't even wear shoes. What is that?'

I shrugged. I didn't know. I just knew that us mission kids were good and left it at that. That was just the way it was. We certainly did a lot of running around back on the community, but what kid didn't? We had to run when flogging mangoes from someone else's backyard without their permission. We had to run if we were in trouble with our elders or anyone else for that matter. We had to run from dogs on our tails. Running and running fast was normal.

Giving up on getting an answer that made even remote sense to her, she sprinted after a couple of her mates making their way over to the tuckshop.

'I'll see ya later,' she called back to me.

'Yeah, see ya.'

'Hey Fiona?' She had stopped and turned back towards me.

With a subtle upward motion of the head and an accompanying raising of the eyes I signalled for her to continue on with her question. This particular white girl made a point of hanging out with us black kids and so understood the subtle, non-verbal communication we used among ourselves.

'I wanna win just one race come sports day. Okay? Just let me win one race.' And with that she was off.

It was true. Most of us mob won the majority of everything on sports day. The main sports the white kids were good at were tennis and swimming, but everything else was dominated by us, particularly athletics and basketball. The latter had been a big part of my childhood. From the age of eight onwards I played in basketball competitions until I left for Sydney when I was sixteen years old – and even then I'd play it with my sisters and cousins on my occasional visits back home. The sweat, the competition, the sound of the whistle blowing, the stress about transport to get to and from the courts at Nanum, the fights on court, contesting the suspensions for fighting, the bright lights beaming down on us, the frozies and hotdogs, families cheering from the sides, the sound of the soles of our shoes squeaking across the courts, the three-pointers and the ever-increasing need to perfect the lay-up were part of the exciting culture of the court. I'm not sure if basketball is embraced back in Weipa now as much as it was during the seventies, eighties and nineties. Certainly none of my daughters have this experience in their lives and this saddens me. This kind of active and passionate competition is undoubtedly beneficial for the mind, body and spirit. I knew, though, that I didn't only want to be good on the track and field; I also wanted to be good on the stage and in the classroom.

'All talent and no brains' was a comment all too often made about us kids from the mission by frustrated whitefellas. The majority of mission kids did not speak much in the classroom but on the tracks was where it was all said and done. I not only loved performing and excelling in sports, but also didn't mind work in the classroom. I got expressive satisfaction out of art, immense enjoyment out of English and challenges out of French. In fact, I enjoyed French so much in Year 9 that throughout Year 10 I took it independently – not as part of a class. Maths and home economics, however, I never really did have the knack for.

I respected everything I did at school, everything. However, I absolutely hated having to travel to school in the ugly big shame job old blue-and-white bus. That bus would splutter and cough all the way into town and back home every day. It was like it was the great-granny of buses. The seats were in the most derelict state. The vinyl had been cut open and the seat stuffing dug out or shredded. Poorly spelled threats and insults lined the walls and backs of the seats, along with explicit drawings of private parts in various positions. The bus was in such an appalling state that I wondered how could they expect anyone to look forward to going to school when this was what greeted them every morning. How the authorities overlooked this was confusing to me. Didn't they care how the youth of the community were presented? It was downright depressing, to say the least, and I found it embarrassingly painful arriving at school this way. I felt quite alone and self-conscious even though most of us kids on that bus every day were related.

I was so aware of the taunts from the white kids as well as some of the more well-to-do black town kids who I thought had no shame by looking down on other blacks. I felt that they should've known better than to act as if they were superior to us. I put their attitude down to the fact that they didn't know where in Weipa they fitted in as people of colour. In my opinion they appeared to have no sense of identity. At least we had our traditional affiliation to the land and weren't pretending to be something we weren't.

We were proud of who we were. Even the Torres Strait Islander kids who lived on Napranum had an identity. They were the TSI Napranumites. Napranum was the only place or home they knew. They spoke not only their own creole but Napranum home-language as well. And even though there was a divide between the Napranum Torres Strait Islander community and the Aboriginal people due to basic and obvious differences between the two, there were also ties as relationships slowly grew between the two races as a result of cross-cultural marriage and interbreeding.

Throughout my childhood I soon became aware that there existed a mentality that because we were from the mission we were somehow inferior to those that lived in town.

The physical fights between us kids from Napranum and the Weipa township mob were all too constant for comfort. These were not little cat fights or just name calling, but full-on blood-drawing punch-ups. Most were the result of either a white girl looking at a black girl the wrong way or for a second too long, or for appearing to make a snide comment about her to her circle of friends. Whatever the case, it almost always ended up in a school-yard fight. I never did enjoy being witness to these – I found them quite disturbing, as I really did get on with everyone and basically minded my own business. I was more interested in doing well both academically and in sport. I wanted a life of being able to live the way I wanted, where it wouldn't always be other people who had the nice houses or nice things. Deep down I felt that if I could make it in school then my life would somchow change.

One time, however, I ended up in the biggest knuckle-up with a white boy. It was in Year 9 or 10, during an art class. All us girls from Naps were sitting around the one table, as we usually did, while the white and black girls from town were positioned at their own tables. This white boy walked past the classroom and, idiotically, said something annoying through the windows. Apparently one of the Torres Strait Islander girls then said something back to him. I'm not sure what words were exchanged as my head was down and I was focused on my work. I loved art and still do. Actually, we all loved art; it was one of the few subjects that us Naps kids felt comfortable in. Anyway, by the time I catch on there's this war of words taking place and next thing I know the white boy spits the words 'you black slut' at her.

Everyone just gasped. There was a five-second pause, which felt like the longest time, then I had to go and make it my business.

'Don't call her a slut. She not a slut and who do you think you are calling her black?'

'Yeah?' he responded, cocking his head from side to side. 'Well whatcha gonna do about it, hey?'

Everyone's eyes were on me – the quiet focused one who never went out of her way to make trouble for herself. But I sure as hell wasn't a pushover either. They waited for a response from me.

One girl pushed for one: 'Oh Fiona, toooo bahhd sissy, 'im be say what you goo do? Stiffen 'im!'

Uh oh, I'm in too deep now, I thought to myself. I've gotta respond somehow and respond fast. I just opened my mouth and let anything drift off my tongue.

'I'm gonna, I'm gonna . . . smush you that's what I'm gonna do,' I said as confidently as I could manage.

'Yeah, well let's see you try.'

And with that he made his way in through the classroom

door and stood there with both arms out, exposing his chest area. I had no choice. No backing out now. I placed my paintbrush down and walked toward him. He didn't know what to expect and just kept staring. I plunged my right arm under his crotch and grabbed the back of his shirt just under his neck with my left. In a split second I'd flipped him onto his back. I sat on top locking my legs around him to keep him pinned down, all the while saying that this girl was not a black slut!

It wasn't too long before our teacher arrived and pulled me off. The boy didn't come to school for about three or four weeks. I was bent over, sipping water from the cooler when I noticed a pair of joggers behind me. I turned around. The boy was standing there, sporting the saddest eyes I've ever seen on a whitefella.

'Uhm, I came to say I'm sorry for calling that girl a black slut.'

'Yeah well, she not a slut, and you shouldn't be calling girls names like that.'

'Yeah I know.'

I just looked at him.

'And I'm sorry for having a go at you.'

I still didn't say anything.

'My sister's sending me away to boarding school. I won't be coming here no more.'

I nodded in acknowledgement and he turned to walk away.

'Hey Tim,' I called out.

'Yeah?'

'Thanks for apologising.'

'No worries.'

And with that the matter was resolved. I never saw him again.

CHAPTER FIVE

'What is it? Is it a woman ghost?'

'No, it's a spirit, my guardian.'

'What's it guarding you against? Why do you have to be guarded?'

'Well anything, I bin do business and I bin do well and now I got this woman spirit to follow me around and guide and warn me 'bout stuff.'

Why a woman spirit? I think to myself. Why not a man spirit as a guide?

During one of our visits to Aurukun, as per usual, we had gone bush for the day, catching a lift with a council vehicle that would return to pick us up at dusk. The adults were gone. Men one way while the women another. Normally us kids would've been required to accompany the adults to assist in hunting and gathering, but every so often we would do our own thing. This was one of those times.

Thomo, a cousin of ours, had started to train spiritually from a young age. He had been through 'men's business' and was well immersed in the spirit world by the time he was about thirteen years old. He had been exposed to the dealings within the supernatural realm and had begun to receive special and certain attributes as a result. His boyishness, however, overrode the purpose of initiation (to recruit him into manhood) and he continued to make time to hang out with his female cousins. When not in training he would occasionally and unlawfully reveal the secrets of men's business to us. Bewildered, us girls would probe him further, with question after question, constantly hungry to know about what goes on in the spirit world. It hadn't occurred to us that this cousin would have to find a balanced way to walk the two realms in order to stay sane, safe and healthy for the rest of his life.

One day we really pestered him. 'What does the woman look like?'

'She floats and got proper long white hair.'

'Is she pretty?'

He shrugged, appearing slightly uncomfortable. 'Aah, I don't know.'

'Does she talk?'

'Not like we talking now. But she talks to me in her mind and I can hear what she saying.'

'Wow, can you talk to her in your mind?'

'I think so, I never really took notice. But I know she listens to me cos she comes when I call her.' He paused briefly, contemplating, and then continued on. 'So she must can hear me.'

'Is she white or black?'

Thomo looked at me, puzzled. 'I don't know.' He appeared slightly agitated.

'Leave that talk about the woman ghost now. Let's go play,' one of my sisters called out. She bolted off to a nearby tree and with one swing she was on her way up. The rest of us ran behind her like a pack of wild brumbies and climbed up.

I sat in the tree with my feet dangling over the branch, digesting the information just released to us. I tried to imagine this woman spirit. She sounded beautiful, mystifying and I wanted to see and meet her. Part of me wanted her to be *my* guide. But according to our cousin, she had to be earned through business practice, through initiation. Besides, I was a girl and there was no way I'd be exposed to her or come even close to an affiliation of any sort. This was secret privileged business, reserved only for initiated males. When you cross over into the supernatural realm without appropriate protection you are subjected to a curse of some sort. This could be caused by too much exposure to the supernatural realm (through sight, knowledge or dealings of some sort). If I were to overstep the boundaries there would be no doubt that the consequences would include illness on my part. I wanted to know if there was business for us girls. Maybe we could earn our own guide and she could follow us wherever we went and look after us as well. I called out to Thomo.

'Say something to her now. Ask her to come visit us, quick!'

'No don't!' yelled one of the other girls as she swung from branch to branch. 'That's not how it's done, Fay. We might get sick.'

'Orr,' I sulked, disappointed.

'She first came to me at Watson. Now she follows me everywhere I go,' Thomo explained.

'Tell us what you can do now,' I pleaded.

'Maybe one day. I can't tell you too much.'

'Why not?'

'Because it could become dangerous.'

'Why?'

'Just because.'

'But why?' I persisted.

'Don't you listen?' Sue interrupted, appearing increasingly agitated. 'Stop pestering him.'

'Can you fly or make yourself invisible?' I continued on, ignoring her.

'I'll yarn later,' Thomo promised. '*Kun ah*. Leave it now.'

I wondered exactly what kind of business he went through. I knew it was men's business but I was curious about the details. It set him apart, made him special, unique and clever. He was about the same age as me and yet he was gaining all this secret knowledge and learning how to practise and function in the spirit realm. There was something about the ability to function between the two realms that excited me.

One time Thomo had been visiting us back at Napranum when it was raining and stormy. I was about fourteen years old and I needed to get back to Nan's place. Standing on the back kitchen veranda at Mum's I could see Thomo on the front veranda leaning slightly over the railing facing north. He was moving his hands around as if flying a kite. There was a lot of lightning around. I couldn't help but get the feeling that he had something to do with the lightning play that afternoon. The apparent synchronicity between the lightning strikes and his arm movements got me thinking.

'Hey, what you doing?' I called out.

'Playing, Fay.'

I shot him a look that was a cross between confused, scared and excited.

More lightning! And thunder. It sounded as if it was right in front of us.

'That's not you . . . is it . . . is that you?' I slowly asked, pointing up.

Thomo nodded.

I gasped. I couldn't really make sense of it. Then I snapped back to reality. I really needed to get home soon. Nan would be worried about my whereabouts and I'd end up copping it.

'I need to get home, stop playing for a while.'

'Alright, hurry up. Start running. I'll hold it until you get there.'

I shot him a doubtful look.

'Go on, it's alright. You'll be right.' Thomo motioned for me to get going.

I bolted down the back kitchen stairs and sprinted across the wet grass blanketed with puddles of rain water then over the bitumen road and up the stairs to 1 Peppan Street. I jumped up on the veranda railings so that Thomo could see me and waved frantically to signal I'd gotten there. He waved back and then *crash*, another lightning bolt let loose.

By the time I was fourteen or fifteen years old I was well immersed in the spiritual and supernatural. They were common, everyday parts of life in our world. Spirits were among us, walked with us, spoke to us and interacted with us. It was not unusual at all. We'd have to watch out for spirits as much as for the bad person physically wrapped up in flesh, blood and bone. Not leaving your clothes hanging on the line after dark, spitting on your pee after you went in the bush, sprinkling salt on your windowsill or under your bed or placing a cup of water under your bed were among many practices we were taught as protection against the bad spirits that roamed about looking for victims. And introducing yourself to the spirits of ancestors and old people when visiting deserted or significant parts of country was something that had been demonstrated consistently to us by the adults, Nan in particular.

'You can get sick or old people will follow us home and steal the youngest one if you don't warn them we there. Old people will be curious and will want to follow us home.' Nan would say. 'So just let them know you in the area out of respect. You listen?'

'Yes, Nan.'

'And always check a person's fingernails, Fay.'

'Why, what for?'

'Well, that's a telltale sign that person knows business. Black fingernails mean that person's been up to no good. They can put their hand in your belly without you knowing or even seeing them. They will muck up your insides, sometimes leaving a rotten fingernail behind.'

'What will they do with my insides?'

Her voice would drop and she'd tell me about what these clever people would do with my blood. My eyes would widen in shocked disbelief as I tried to make sense of what I'd just heard. Knowing this always sent shivers up me. Still, I always checked people's fingernails, even those who were family. When I noticed a relative with black fingernails I'd go to Nan and report it.

'It's alright, just be careful. That uncle is trained,' she'd say. Or 'that old-fella know that business but you'll be alright.'

Yeah I hope so, I would think to myself. How can we be truly sure?

Nan also revealed to me the role that the plant known commonly as blackboy plant or spear grass tree played during *Idwira* or men's business. She told me as much as she possibly could.

'*Oolay Omb*, that's what it's called among the Alngith. *Oolay Omb* is an ancestral totem to the Alngith. Whitefellas use it for decoration. We use it in spiritual warfare and activity.'

Mum had plenty to teach us too. She told us girls about her guardians that Grandad sang into manifestation. Two *noombathies* they were and the closest description for a *noombathi* is your belly button. These two were Mum's guardians and would take care of her no matter where she went. One was red and the other blue. Mum said that the other villagers would often see them as lights in and around the house at night.

Grandad had been through appropriate business to be able to sing to these two spirit guides. I had been told that he had to be swallowed by a spirit crocodile and go through dream ceremony in order to acquire the ability to see into the short-term future. Although, once Grandad started drinking – and progressed onto rum in particular – his ability was taken away from him. He no longer had a strong, clear mind and a spirit belly.

Several years into my double digits I was caught by song magic. Something that had been intended for someone else (or so I told myself, as who would've intentionally wanted to harm me?)

found its way straight into my head and lodged itself in the back of my right ear. The pain had manifested soon after returning back home to Naps following one of our frequent visits to Aurukun. Now, in community life physical fist fights and brawls can get frighteningly huge, often taking up a vast amount of space as people slowly moved en masse from one end of the community to the other, quite literally. Today, the very thought of this sickens me, but, as a child, the very hint of a fight taking place spelled entertainment. Immediately I'd be swept along in the stream of wannabe spectators. This particular time, most probably in the late afternoon going on early evening, a big fight between families had broken out. The adults warned us kids not to wander too far into the middle of the brawling crowd; these fights had the potential to get extremely serious, with various kinds of weaponry being flung around. As usual, the adults' warnings and threats entered into one ear and immediately went out the other. This day, I entered the fight space and positioned myself in the front row with both arms crossed in front of me. The shouting, insults, threats and crying, all mostly in Munkun echoed around me. People were barely recognisable as darkness fell, but they continued to drift around in the madness.

By the time us kids got home it must've been quite late, at least 11 pm if not midnight. In the days following this fight I noticed a dull ache in my ear. The pain slowly built up over a week and by the seventh or eighth day it had consumed most of the right side of my head. The thumping and heaviness hurt so badly that I could not even react to it. I would just lay there, almost delirious, wishing to just fall into deep sleep and not wake up at all.

One Sunday, Nan had decided to get me up. She made me shower and accompany her on the twenty-minute walk to the church for prayer. The singing did bring a sort of peace to me for a while, but as soon as I got back home the pain returned with such intensity that I felt ready to give my spirit up and slip peacefully into the afterlife. Eventually, a particular grandfather was called in to perform ceremony on me. I barely had the strength to make my way out onto the veranda and position myself at the top end of it, as certain family members sat nearby for support. The old healer first placed smell from his armpits on my head to protect me as he had been through business and was an initiated man. He then placed his mouth on my neck and after each suck would spit out over the veranda. He informed Nan that I had been 'caught through song business' and that, indeed, there was something in my head although he was not exactly sure which area it was in.

He placed his mouth over my left ear and sucked. Nothing. On turning his attention to my right ear he backed away. He had found the cause of my pain. I wondered why he did not start with my right ear in the first place as it had been clearly pointed out to him that that was where the pain was. Anyway, his mouth now enveloped my right ear and with each suck I could feel something moving in an outward direction. Several sucks later he spat something into the air and returned the curse back to where it came from. I later learnt that he had returned the cursed object back to the person responsible. It had been a silver song marble which had lodged deep in my ear canal. It had been sung with the intent to slowly but surely destroy. How long I had left is a mystery to this day, although I prefer to not think about it. I did wonder why prayer hadn't healed me. Regardless, my faith in the God of the Bible was not in any way shaken.

CHAPTER SIX

By Year 10 I was becoming more conscious of social status. More than ever I realised the class divide, forever making comparisons about money, speech, dress, behaviour, living conditions, lifestyle and hobbies. How we lived our lives always, for some reason, felt like a lower standard of living than those who lived in the Weipa township. And even though I had the best childhood ever, and I loved my families and my people, I wanted more. I wanted what the white kids had, what the well-to-do black families had. Shame and embarrassment about my background slowly began to seep in and overtake my thinking, how I felt and my approach to life. I began to look at ways of exiting this hole of despair. I wanted out, out of Napranum, out from being a mission kid at school, out from travelling on that gammon old bus every day. I felt that I deserved *more*, that something, somewhere along the line, had gone awry, that I was caught up in the wrong social class somehow. I wanted to separate myself from this particular class.

Basically, I did not want to be considered, or feel, like a poor loser underdog.

No matter where I was I felt like an outcast. Gone was that comfortable sense of belonging that I had in primary school. Now that I had some awareness of social settings and status I felt that I was living a life that became unacceptable. I cringed whenever Nan or Mum came to the school. I hated it! I felt that a big spotlight was on me and that everyone would know that I didn't have a *normal* family – a mum, a dad and siblings in a neat little house. Don't get me wrong, I loved my family and was extremely proud of my grandmother and feared and respected her, but my fast developing social perceptions had robbed me of continuing to see the unique situation that had always been an ongoing support and blessing to me no matter what hardships we had endured as a family along the way.

Around this time I began to wonder about my father. The white man whose name was the only thing I knew about him. Where was he? He was biologically the other half of me. I wanted to know him, as perhaps in knowing him I would begin to discover my whole self. I felt like half a person in almost every respect, but I mostly kept silent. My thinking and my ways were different to my family's. I loved to sit and watch old European movies, especially the ones from Italy and Germany. There was something about the people, the way they spoke and the way they looked that caught and held my attention. But I never spoke to anyone about this side of me; there was no-one I could'vc spoken to. It would've been disrespectful to keep expressing an interest in my *other* sense of identity.

During the late seventies when I was about nine years old a dance team from the Sydney-based Aboriginal and Islander Dance Theatre visited Napranum. AIDT had grown out of Black Theatre and had been established in 1976 as a full-time training program with the aim of creating opportunities for Indigenous people to have careers in professional dance. Carole Johnson, its founder, had originally come to Australia as part of the Eleo Pomare Dance Company in 1972. She was asked by the Australia Council to stay on and work with Aboriginal people in dance, with workshops first being held in the St James Church hall in Glebe.

I remember that first dance session in Napranum quite clearly. The instructors were Richard Talonga and Lillian Crombie and a couple more. The song we danced to was *We Are Family* by the Pointer Sisters and I even remember some of the choreography they taught us that day. I could not take my eyes off Lillian, this beautiful black girl standing up the front in leotard and tights. I had never seen a black girl dressed like this before, ever. Here was this girl, same as us, dressed in a way that no-one in the community did. That caught my attention.

The chiselled physique of Richard Talonga may have had some sort of impact on me that day as well. His sharp muscles rippled every time the guy moved. Richard had absolutely amazing flexibility. He was truly unique and an exceptional dancer. He moved with agility and possessed a stealthy way of moving that is quite rare even among dancers. What he had was something that no amount of training could bring. You had to be born with it. I'm sure all us girls at the Jessica Point State School that day were totally dazzled by his presence; well, I was anyway. And Lillian's smile just radiated. Even today, Lillian Crombie has that same smile. She has this look that is just infectious. During that particular class I made a decision that would permanently alter the direction of my life. From that moment on, dance, in a contemporary sense, would always embrace me and I, in turn, would embrace it.

My next encounter with dance in a formal training sense was several years later when I was in Year 9. Our English teacher realised a few of us were interested in dance and organised a handful of us mission kids to participate in jazz classes once a week at the house on the hill, a building several hundred metres down the road from the high school where dance classes, and occasionally discos, were held. I thoroughly enjoyed this opportunity. There was no way us kids would've been able to experience anything like this otherwise. Opportunities like that just weren't possible, not for a mission kid. For the first time ever I was introduced to the barre as well as the mirror. And there was no shame associated with looking at yourself. I soon realised I could check myself out as much as I wanted to. It was connected to the class, not to being vain or up myself. I loved that freedom. For the first time I learnt about isolated arm rotations, head circulations, leg rotations and placement. Skips, jumps and runs across the floor were all now part of an exciting new movement vocabulary. I was participating in a class like the ones I had seen on films, such as *Fame* and *Flashdance*. This indeed was exciting stuff and I was getting hooked, fast.

Shortly afterwards there was a trip to Cairns to attend another workshop hosted by AIDT. By now I was deadset on following through with a career in dance and drama. I was involved in our school plays, which was unusual for us mission kids, but I really wanted to try out this acting thing that I'd seen the white kids doing. It felt as though things were falling into place as these small openings presented to me, and my family did not seem to object. Mum and Nan appeared to respect my choice to be involved with dance and performing, although surely they noticed that my interest in athletics and basketball had begun to take a back seat.

The end of Year 10 saw four of us girls from school make the trip from Napranum to Sydney, our first big city experience. Tony Boxer from Napranum and Aunty Sylvia Blanco from town were already associated with AIDT. That was all I needed to know to keep me focused and keep believing that a career in dance was indeed very possible. I didn't need to be able to do eleven pirouettes already like Mikhail Baryshnikov did in *White Nights*. Nor did I have to be able to split in the air during a jeté across the floor or be *en pointe* like those girls in the dance magazines that I'd skim through at the house on the hill. No, they would take me as I was and I would use the training. As long as I was prepared to work hard, I would get there, wherever *there* was.

Our English teacher helped us with our applications and before long I had been accepted to participate in the AIDT auditions scheduled for November 1984. I was fourteen years old, technically not old enough to even audition, let alone do the course. I had intentionally withheld my true age. And obviously Mum and Nan weren't quite up to speed at the time because somehow I got away with it and made the auditions. Oh my goodness, landing in a city the size of Sydney at the age I was, first time out of an isolated community in the Cape was overwhelming. I felt both scared and excited. We had left our safe little home in the Cape in the morning during daylight and arrived in this huge monster city when it was dark. As a small child I had always wished for a chance to travel to Sydney, and here I was. We stayed somewhere in Glebe, and were driven around in a blue-and-white coaster bus. We were taken shopping for leotards, tights, ballet shoes, leg warmers (just like Jennifer Beals in *Flashdance*) and what were known as kung-fu shoes for tap. These were cotton slip-ons with rubber soles. Getting to know other like-minded, interesting and sometimes crazy *Flashdance* and *Fame* wannabes was exciting indeed. But I struggled my way through the two weeks at the barre and on the floor, and then during the final presentation. I had neither flexibility nor grace and I was as uncoordinated as a blind dog with three left feet. In fact, I wasn't that good at all! Despite realising this I was still quite upset upon learning that I had *not* been accepted into AIDT for the following year. Only one out of the four of us who auditioned was accepted. She excitedly packed and returned to Sydney to begin her training while I reluctantly prepared for my return to school.

I quickly immersed myself back into school culture at Weipa High. The sporting competitions, the need to excel academically and a handful of boys held my interest throughout that year and the year flew by. The whole time, though, I knew that I would return to Sydney at the end of that year to re-audition. The official age to audition at AIDT was seventeen and here I was not quite sixteen auditioning with focused zeal for the second time. Nobody was gonna turn me down this time if I could help it. Nan and Mum once more appeared oblivious to the age factor. They were happy that I had opted to return to school. But it was appearing more and more obvious to me that my heart was for dance and the first opportunity I had to leave the community would have me out of there. After successfully completing Year 11, I was off once more.

I had seen enough inspirational dance films to keep me fuelled for a long time. Michael Jackson's *Thriller* was out by now as well and anyone who had the slightest interest in dance wanted to be able to do the combination choreography the funky corpses performed in that clip. I knew, too, that I wanted to wear a leotard and tights along with a matching headband and leg warmers. That was the look. It was the ultimate excitement for a little black girl from Napranum to dress like that.

My persistence paid off.

By then I had tasted physical floggings off both my grandmother and my mum all too often. At fourteen, I had been whipped until the skin on my arms and back sported thick purple slashes and swelling that lasted for weeks. I clearly remember Lyn crying and yelling to *please stop* that *Fay had had enough* and to *please leave her alone*. Later that day I lay naked on my tummy on the lounge room floor while someone gently rubbed coconut oil over my raw strapped flesh. All this because of a yarn told to them about me that wasn't even true. I realise now that neither my mum nor my nan knew how to appropriately deal with issues that were emotionally or socially challenging. Picking up that belt or stick was their only option. I harbour no resentment though, quite the opposite.

I turned sixteen in January 1985 and set off for Sydney not long after that, eager to commence my formal training at AIDT and without asking Nan or Mum for their permission. I told them that I was going and that was that. They probably realised that my mind was set and there would've been no point trying to deter me. I was leaving behind all that was familiar, all that I had known, all that I loved.

I have very little memory of 1985, my first year of formal dance training at Naisda (formerly known as AIDT). Accommodation was at the Chicka Dixon Hostel at Enfield in Sydney's inner west. The room I shared with two other girls was fairly large. Three single beds were positioned in a way that allowed enough space for us to move freely. These girls appeared to be close friends and probably just made way for me simply because I was younger. One of the girls was from Napranum, so she may have felt obligated to look out for me considering we came from the same home town. But I felt safe with these girls playing the big sister role. It gave me a sense of family during a time when I had really needed it.

The Chicka Dixon Aboriginal Hostel catered for up to twelve students from all over Australia, mainly those who were studying the Naisda dance course. It was named after an Aboriginal activist and leader who had spent his lifetime fighting for basic human rights and justice for all Aboriginal and Torres Strait Islander people. Chicka Dixon was born in 1928 and grew up at the Aboriginal mission on Wallaga Lake in New South Wales. The hostel parents, Teddy and Kerry Mundine, were gentle and quiet and mostly tended to their own family business. But they were always there to meet the constant needs of the students both collectively and individually wherever and whenever necessary.

I struggled my way through that first year both physically and socially. I was sixteen years old and even though up until that point

I was focused and possessed a strong spirit, for some reason I felt awkward and, well, just not that popular. I became very aware of the talents and capabilities of the other students and consistently felt like I could never measure up to them, although I must admit I still felt I had a quiet inner strength. This kept me going and carried me through the majority of my training years at Naisda and beyond.

That first year in Sydney meant bus trips to and from our dance school and contending with the rigorous training and exercises we were required to undergo every day, eight hours a day, five days a week. As a first-year student I was on a fortnightly allowance of about $140 and after paying rent, which equated to about $70 per fortnight, purchasing necessary toiletries and a weekly bus pass, and fulfilling the desire to add to my wardrobe there'd probably be about $30 left to spend on fun activities like weekend trips to Luna Park, before my next payment came around. The extra allowance of $200 that Nan would occasionally send to me would absolutely make my day. How she was able to afford this back then I do not know, but I would foolishly spend this money – equivalent these days to about $1000 – on clothes, clothes and more clothes.

During that first year I kept finding poems addressed to me in or near my bag. At first I thought it was a joke or that the poems were meant for someone else until the mystery poet revealed himself to me. Unfortunately, I did not feel the same way about this boy and the poems, as sweet as they were, failed to convince me otherwise. The boy's attention quickly switched to someone else who, lucky for him, responded favourably. There wasn't anyone I was interested in – overwhelmed as I was at the complete change of environment and pace. There was so much to focus on in terms of discipline and commitment to my dance studies. Who had time to get involved with a boy? Besides no-one had really caught my eye. I was flat out just getting out of bed in the morning and making it to school on time. It was always a bit of a stretch surviving the long, physically gruelling days. Classes usually went for one and a half to two hours, particularly the modern and classical, but thankfully our day was broken up by scheduled music, cultural and political studies and the continuation of basic math and English classes. Committing to this demanding lifestyle was, for a sixteen-year-old, definitely an eye-opener.

And if that wasn't enough, I suddenly discovered the freedom of partying in the big city. The endless selection of nightclubs kept us going constantly. And the selection of clothes – oh my goodness – I had never before been exposed to so much choice in my life. What's more, there wasn't anyone around to spy on me or tell me what to do. Suddenly I was in the largest city in Australia and I could do whatever I wanted, whenever I wanted. But my body was being worked in a way that it never had been prior to this. It was almost as if all that running in the bush, swimming in the creeks and competition basketball throughout my childhood were only preparation for my introduction to the world of professional dance. The physical challenges on my body had obviously gone up a gear. That year I was introduced to modern ballet (Horton, Cunningham and Graham techniques), jazz and Afro jazz, classical and tap. What a smorgasbord of styles to feast on.

There was a particularly odd-shaped room at the top of the stairs just across from my bedroom. I had always thought that this room had a very strong energy whenever I had entered it. It was so small there wasn't any room for a bed; instead, there was a raised section where a mattress could go. The first time I walked into this room I got a very powerful feeling that this raised area represented a coffin or something similar. I knew that no-one should spend time in this room let alone sleep in it, and made a note to steer clear of it. A fellow student who decided to give it a go did not last long. He told us that when he slept on the bed he felt he was sinking or dying and that there was definitely a spirit inhabiting that room. I always felt that the spirit inhabited the entire hostel, as students kept experiencing various spiritual encounters throughout that year.

My most significant spiritual encounter happened one night while I was asleep. At the time I'm pretty sure the other girls weren't there in our room. As soon the spirit arrived at the door I woke up. I watched it make its way over toward me, although not with my physical eye. It sat on the side of my bed and gently placed its hand on me. By this stage I had rolled onto my back and was looking straight at it. There was no obvious face to this spirit, but I sensed a curious, gentle energy emanating from it. The spirit stroked my body ever so gently several times and lifted up the upper section of my body from time to time. It was as if there was a subtle sexual energy in the room, but at sixteen what did I know about sex and its energy?

Dancewise, our focus for the year was working toward our end-of-year production, *Trackin*. I absolutely loved the process of learning and constructing a piece of choreography, rehearsing with some thirty-odd students and then making the shift from the studio to the stage and experiencing all the other demands of performance – costume fittings, lights, make-up. It was all very exciting, and to this day I love the sound, smell and atmosphere of the theatre during rehearsal and performance time; it satisfies my insides. As a first-year dance student, though, I sat back and watched the older students rehearsing their pieces. I really looked up to them. They were inspiring. Names like Delores Scott, Gail Mabo, Marilyn Miller and Stephen Page come to mind. Even the girl from back home had grown considerably in her stage presence and ability to execute movement powerfully. I learnt so much from each and every one of the dancers who had commenced their training before me.

By the end of that first year, however, and for a reason I cannot recall, I decided not to return to Naisda. All I ever wanted to do was leave Napranum and train to become a performer, and yet here I was, about to turn seventeen, wanting to return home. I must've been either very exhausted or lonely or both to just leave like that. Whatever it was, on wrapping up our performance season of *Trackin* I packed my bags.

The yellow cascara flowers and the orange Christmas flowers, as they were commonly known, made for a truly welcoming moment as the plane landed at Cairns airport. I knew I was home. I had missed this environment so much in the past twelve months and now just wanted to breathe, eat and smell the land I loved. On exiting the plane, I noticed the way the sun stroked my skin and blanketed my body. The breeze rolled in from the ocean as if silently welcoming me. And, although I had just spent the year among other Indigenous students from all over Australia, to see my own people all around me again and hear the familiar Indigenous vernaculars being spoken was like honey to my belly – even though home was still another 800 kilometres further north.

Not long after my arrival back in Weipa I became associated with the local community council. Nan had been a councillor for some time and was extremely active in local community affairs and politics for as long as I could remember. From around eleven or twelve years old I'd had various jobs, including working at the butcher, the store and the Department of Community Services office. These positions had me cleaning, stacking shelves and answering phones. Now both my sister Lynette and I worked at the council office and it wasn't long before I found myself a role as payroll trainee. At seventeen years old I was responsible for handling quite substantial amounts of money on a weekly basis. There were a few of us girls learning the ropes and we were responsible for the day-to-day running of the council chambers that year. Belphina Wapau, Patsy Hudson, Laura Pitt and Jackie Madua made up the Naps council team, along with Lynette and I, and we received training in housing, payroll, front desk and other basic office duties. Although I was back to small community living, it was a fun year.

Here I was earning a lot more than I had ever been used to but lots of money plus adolescent hormones minus guidance from elders made for some careless decision-making, misuse of my finances, and frequent attendances at alcohol-fuelled parties and discos. Gone, suddenly, was the ability to uphold the wise teachings that my nan had instilled in me throughout my childhood. Smoking, drinking and stylin' up became my priorities and I had very little concern for the possible risks I was exposing myself to. Still, my sister and I were both gaining an independent life for ourselves. Lyn, who by this stage had turned twenty-one, was given a house next to the training centre where she was now an office attendant, and a good friend at the time agreed to act as guarantor for us so that we could buy our very first car. Up until this point our family had never owned a car. We had always depended on relatives, the council or public transport. We were so proud of our little brown Datsun. However, our pride and joy, and the convenience of owning our own wheels, was destined to be short-lived. We ended up at a party at Lake Patricia late one night after a disco, as was the norm. People were just sitting around in groups drinking, dancing, hooking up and carrying on, as you do. I was sitting in the front passenger side of the car listening to music while one of my younger sisters and her friend were in the back. Suddenly this boy who was quite intoxicated and probably stoned opened the door to the driver's side and slid in. Unfortunately, we had left the keys in the ignition.

'I'm gonna take youse for a drive and I'm gonna crash this car,' he slurred.

At first I did not take him seriously.

'Don't be stupid, turn the car off and give me the keys.'

His response was to put the car straight into second gear and fishtail off down the winding gravel road. Now anyone who is familiar with the roads along Lake Patricia and Lake McLeod knows how bad they can get – a mixture of potholes and bull dust. Within seconds the girls and I were bracing ourselves for the inevitable crash. All I can remember now are the screams from the girls in the back seat and then silence. This boy had lost control of the car and we had flipped and landed upside down. Everything was quiet after the impact, the only sound was the wheels still spinning. For a moment I thought that maybe we were all dead, but then I realised I could move. Suddenly my sister and her friend started looking for a way to exit the car through the windows. Not long after that a car arrived from the party. By this stage our Evel Knievel wannabe had fled the scene for fear of getting flogged. Our beloved car was a total write-off, but here we were with a car loan still to pay off. I will never forget the look of pure disappointment on Mum's face when she realised what had happened. It had been only weeks since we had bought that Datsun.

That incident aside, it was really empowering for both Lyn and I to share our first place together. By this stage I had moved out of Nan's place and in with Lyn. It was fun shopping for second-hand furniture at garage sales in town and doing the place up the way we liked it. Good friends of ours lived next door and were very supportive. These two were always there for us whenever we needed anything. We'd babysit their three children in return.

Onc day I was napping in my room when I suddenly felt like I was drowning. I could hear noises next door, traffic driving past outside, I could even hear Lyn and her then boyfriend talking in the adjacent room. There was the sensation and sound of water rising slowly from the bottom of my bed up toward my head. I began to panic and felt that if did not wake up soon I would drown. I tried to move but couldn't. I had no control over my limbs and movements, everything was numb. I tried calling out to Lyn but I couldn't even speak. I could feel my heart racing and my breathing getting faster. As the water got closer to my face my fingers and toes began to twitch a little. Just before the water was to engulf me

I managed to jolt myself into a state of consciousness. When I told Lyn about what I had experienced she didn't take me seriously. She just gave me a confused look and went about her business.

During that year I also quickly learnt which male relatives could be trusted and which ones couldn't. I realised how easy it was, especially for older men, to attempt to wander down a certain path and commit business that was inappropriate or downright wrong. It was quite clear they felt that if they could get away with business of a sexual nature then they would go through with it. This happened both in and around the community as well as in the church. It wasn't every single male, but I was always shocked to discover who would reveal that side of themselves towards us young girls. We never told Mum or Nan, or any other adults for that matter, for fear of causing big trouble. We'd just discuss this sort of business among ourselves and keep it hush hush. It was already shame business; we figured that if we highlighted what they were doing it would just make things worse for all involved. The fights that would result from confrontation would become extremely serious.

I did love working at the council chambers though. Us girls had so much fun working in an environment where we had the opportunity to upskill, earn money and contribute back to our people and our community in a positive and constructive way. It really was a good place to be. The vibe in the air right across the community during the mid to late eighties was about the people and their communities gaining control in decision-making, policy-making and implementation and progressing economically and in quality of living. Dialogue between the people and government at regional, state and federal levels was on a roll and issues about traditional ownership, recognition and compensation were in full swing. I remember Nan's ongoing support and participation in the dialogue and process on behalf of families of Peppan Street in terms of appropriate compensation being made to the correctly identified family groups of the area. This area is now known as the RAAF Base Scherger, which was opened in 1998.

We especially enjoyed the frequent visits made by tourists and others. One time *60 Minutes* came to Napranum to do a report on the new Community Development Employment Program (CDEP) that had been implemented into the community. This was a government initiated and funded program that encouraged people to work for the dole. It appeared to be working. Never before had I seen the place come alive and people work together for the benefit of the community as they were. People really started to cooperate and gain workforce skills. Those with natural leadership qualities were identified and appointed to supervisory positions, a tremendous boost to their self-esteem. All round it was a very exciting and busy year for Napranum. The *60 Minutes* people recorded several interviews in and around the community and understandably there was some excitement when the report went to air – there was a clear view of me handing out pay packets to the CDEP workers.

Unbeknown to me, at the same time a group of young Murri boys were sitting around the television set at a boys' hostel in West End, Brisbane, watching the report. In that group was a twenty-year-old Murri fella by the name of Danny Doyle.

'That's my woman there,' he claimed, half laughing and half serious.

The rest of the boys all laughed.

'Yeah, you wish brother,' the others mocked.

'Nah true, I'm gonna marry her one day. Youse wait and see.'

One particular day a tall whitefella cruised into Naps on a motorbike. Now here was a sight not common to the area. Just the sound of the arrival of that bike was enough to create a bit of excitement and get all our hearts pumping. As soon as he entered the office and removed his helmet all us girls just stared at him without saying a word. We had all become familiar with appropriate office etiquette and had no trouble in executing delivery of it, but this particular whitefella soon dispersed that. None of us would attend to him, both out of heart-stopping nerves and shame. I can't remember who ended up addressing his enquiry concerning his unemployment benefit form. As for how I scored a date with him I have no idea.

I spent several weeks seeing this fella and the news quickly spread around Napranum that Fiona George had been seen on the back of a strange, tall whitefella's motorbike. He would take me to various units and flats, where – I did not realise it at the time – he would score drugs and use them right in front of me. We got on reasonably well and conversation was always comfortable, interesting and free-flowing. He came across as a fairly chilled, gentle person so it was all good with me while it lasted. The turning point came when he dropped me off at the bus-stop just up the road from where I lived and prepared to kiss me goodbye for the first time. Up until that point somehow we had avoided contact of a physical or sexual nature. It felt exciting being up against his tall, and sleek body but when his lips met mine there was nothing there – no energy, no thrill, no connection. I went cold immediately, just switched off, really. It wasn't bad but it wasn't good either.

Not long after that I lost interest. He turned up at our place at Callope Street one Saturday morning and persistently knocked. I refused to answer the door. Mum kept saying how rude I was being and that she thought he was a nice enough guy. He must've waited on the veranda for about half an hour just patiently knocking and knocking, while my sisters and cousins kept insisting I take pity on him.

'Don't Fay, poor fella, sorry one. You shouldn't do this to him.'

'Youse have him if you want, go,' I snapped back at them.

I'm not sure if someone ended up going outside and telling him that I didn't want to see him anymore or whether he just decided to leave. Either way, he got on his deadly bike and rode off. I must've been so thick to treat this sexy man in such a way, but I knew very little about relationships back then. He continued to pursue me at the disco, refusing to leave me alone even when I demonstrated my lack of interest. A cousin of mine who lives for fighting asked if I needed help getting a message across to this 'pesky whitefella'. I said he was harmless and that it was all good. My cousin knew that there was more to it than that, but opted to just stand in full view of him until my mystery bike rider got the message and backed off.

That same year a well-known Indigenous basketball player visited Weipa. Once more word got around that this six-foot-something catch was in town and that us girls from the office should go check him out. I was the second-youngest of the group so, naturally, I tagged along thinking that I'd get to party with everyone, but of course if this fella was going to show an interest in anyone it certainly wasn't going to be me. We were in the Sportman's Bar drinking, talking, scanning and flirting, as you do. He towered over people so it wasn't hard to notice him. The first time I looked his way, more out of curiosity than anything, he sent me a smile. Feeling a slight rush of excitement, I returned a nervous little smile but kept talking to the girl I was with. I continued to check out where he was, and to my surprise, even though he was engaged in conversation his sight was firmly on me throughout the evening. I couldn't believe that this fella was sending messages to me. I was a bit embarrassed as the girl I was with had expressed interest in him and was hoping for a hook-up. Eventually he made his way over to where we were just as we were about to leave. Small talk and flirting was good enough for a seventeen-year-old who didn't fully understand what a male in his mid- to late-twenties would probably prefer. I didn't end up with him that night but it was for the best.

The next day, however, I was in the fruit and vegies section at the local Woolworths supermarket with my mum when he walked in. I thought he would not be so bold as to attempt a conversation, but I had underestimated his charm. He yarned with Mum while I quietly stood by. As they wrapped up with the usual 'bye now, good to meet you' line he discreetly slipped me his room and phone number on a small piece of paper.

'What a lovely young fella,' Mum said as she continued with our grocery shopping. 'So tall, handsome and polite.'

What a sneaky fella, was what I was thinking, as I quickly slipped his number into my bra before Mum could notice.

Attending the local disco at the Albatross was high on my list of weekly must-dos. I did anything to be there every Friday night. I loved the buzz of dressing up, turning up, being there and riding the whole wave of drinking, partying and flirting. I had become more strong-headed; gone were the days when Nan and Mum had a say in what I did and how I did it. I simply did my own thing. Throughout 1986 I experimented with a couple of local boys but was never really serious about any of them. Who is at that age, when you really couldn't care less about consequences or what people say or think about you?

I wasn't only learning about parties, discos and eyeing off the next cute boy that came along, though. I was also gaining considerable knowledge about community affairs. I had returned to one of my most-loved sports, basketball, and played in a team with my family. This provided an opportunity to keep fit; maintain my physical stamina; and function in a focused, disciplined and positive manner. It was a good addition to my life, although my hormones must've been on fast forward as I recall some pretty full-on fist fights on court that year. During one game, a quite tall, white local girl in our opposition team had the ball. I placed myself right in front of her and continued to jump and block no matter which way she tried to pivot. I annoyed her so much that suddenly this girl paused for a couple of seconds, looked straight at me with a look of pure exasperation and, cupping the ball firmly with both hands, banged me right in the middle of my face. Now white girls just did not take on the blacks like this, certainly not in such a bold way. I was probably the most stunned out of everyone on court. In a split second though the punches started. I don't think I got more than two or three in when a couple of my sisters took over. All I remember is this white girl bent over with both her hands shielding her face. I almost admired her for what she did to me though.

The next day Mum and Nan went looking for this girl at the shops where she worked as a hairdresser, and, as she tended to a customer, they did to her exactly what the girl did to me. I will say no more.

Physical fights continued and, just as I had throughout primary and high school, I just rode the wave and went with the flow. That was the mentality: you don't walk away, you stay and you fist fight your way through the situation. The older I got the bigger and scarier my opponents became – whether it was fighting off a mob who'd attacked Lynette during an all-night party or fighting off two sisters who had nothing better to do than attack and insult those of us that they had decided were their enemies.

The whole time I was riding this roller-coaster I was aware deep down that this was not where I was supposed to be and this was definitely not how I wanted to live. I wanted out. There was so much more to life, I felt. I had carried on being silly for so much of that year, I knew I just couldn't keep going for another one. It was once more time to get serious and productive about where I was heading. I didn't want to be the teenager that everyone gossiped or told fibs about. I didn't want to keep clarifying yarns to Nan and Mum whenever I got questioned. I didn't want to keep dying my hair blonde every time I got bored. This was stupid living. I thought about the life I had left behind in Sydney. I suppose I could have climbed the ranks within the council and maybe been CEO one day, made lots of money, got fat eating free lunches and dinners at endless council meetings. Who knows? But I knew that was not my thing. My creative, imaginative spirit couldn't wait to get back out of the confines of Napranum, and Weipa.

One afternoon when things were a bit quiet at work I drew up two columns on a piece of paper. To the left was *If I stay in Weipa* and to the right *If I go to Sydney* – the positives and negatives. The positives of staying were that I would remain with family and keep making money. As for the negatives, I just felt that my life would've kept going in a cycle of drinking, partying and fighting – the small town mentality. Returning to Sydney and taking up dance again would no doubt extend me in a way that Napranum wouldn't. It really could be a dream lifestyle, if only I would commit. By the time I'd finished, the positives in the column to the right far outweighed the list on the left.

At the end of 1986 I took the necessary steps towards returning to Naisda. I rang Carole Johnson who, fortunately for me, said that a re-audition was not necessary; I would be able to go straight into second year. Shortly after New Year I boarded the plane for Sydney once more with no resistance from my family. By this stage Lyn was busy with her life, Mum was preoccupied with her marriage and the issues that came with that and Nan continued to focus on community and church. Any sadness and concern she expressed regarding my leaving wasn't enough to hold me back.

I immediately connected with my new dancing group and fell right back into the rigorous training and regime the course demanded. Talk about a wake-up call! It was good that I had kept up with basketball, so at least my body had some fitness and was still quite strong. I was not technically strong though, not at all, and lacked flexibility. I decided early on to work my guts out.

I wanted a toned, strong, flexible physique and the only way to get that was to work hard.

Sydney was a familiar place to me now and my ability to connect with the other students came more freely the second time around. I was eighteen years old, by now, and especially enjoyed forming new friendships.

We lived in a different hostel. The Tony Mundine Hostel in Leichhardt was quite big and I quickly fell into a routine of hostel life: making sure I was on time if I did not want to miss out on dinner, not having a say on what was on the menu, putting up with bad video choices on Friday and Saturday nights in the entertainment room or other people's preferences of what to watch on TV. The noise level was always a force to be reckoned with, as was having to wait your turn to use the toilets and showers. Luckily the bathroom was just across from my room, so I didn't have to walk too far late at night to use them. Imagine the energy in the air from twenty-five to thirty students ranging from eighteen to thirty-five living under the one roof – it was pretty full-on. Surprisingly, it worked the majority of the time and except for the odd fight or disturbance everything pretty much functioned systematically. Again, partying and attending discos, especially along Oxford Street, became the thing to do on weekends. Sue Mundine, our hostel manager, was pretty much on top of everything and had a stern but gentle and effective approach to running the place.

I quickly signed up for weekend cooking and cleaning duties, which earned me an extra couple of hundred of dollars in addition to my ABSTUDY allowance. Friday and Saturday nights in front of the television set due to lack of dollars to fund regular partying led to me forming a relationship with another student from my year. Lenny would crack the driest of jokes. I laughed not at the jokes, but at the fact he was so bad at humour and did not even realise it. At least he was attempting to make me laugh, right? I needed to do much more of that, as I have mostly quite a serious nature.

Sometimes he'd throw rolled up balls of bread at me during our lunch breaks in the park across from the dance school. He would then pretend to be in deep conversation with his circle of friends as I looked about trying to figure out where the ball of bread was coming from. I was aware that he had previously been involved in a relationship with another man, but during the winter months I soon found myself under his doona where we kept each other warm as 'just friends'.

One thing led to another and before I knew it we were frequenting each other's rooms on a regular basis and his company was something I came to enjoy. He had a laugh that was infectious, a spirit that was stubborn, a personality that was headstrong and a six pack that was impressive.

During that year I became quite obsessed with my body. Being as thin and as toned as I could possibly be was my priority. I basically lived on yoghurt and fruit with the occasional rice meal from Chinatown, a payday treat. I ate as little as I could at the hostel. Food was my enemy. I stopped eating bread especially. In any case, I was always doing extra classes at the Sydney Dance Company that our principal modern teacher gave each week, so by the time I got home the kitchen was closed for the night. Before I knew it, my body was used to my not eating as much. I walked between classes and became a regular at the gym on Broadway Street where I did weight training. I also participated a lot in that activity you tend to do with that one particular person you are interested in and enjoy being around, a workout in itself. This lifestyle got me the body I wanted and I maintained this routine for the majority of 1987 and 1988, balancing on about 48 kilos at a height of 163 cm.

When I looked into the mirror during a dance class or workout all I wanted to see was a thin, toned body. A number of the other girls also seemed to be obsessing about their shape and size. Extreme and unhealthy eating habits became more evident. Wrapping cling wrap under heavy clothing to increase sweating and burn fat was something that not only us girls had taken up but a couple of the boys as well. The slow sipping of Milo and nothing much else replaced a healthy diet and, consequently, those who opted for this approach were often literally passing out at the barre mid-session. Life had become a matter of who looked good and who was sleeping with who and for how long.

That year, too, the fighter in me reared its dumb head once more. Our dance group consisted of four boys and myself. We had been working through a piece in Studio 2 downstairs when something sparked off a disagreement and before I knew it I was locked in a tongue bash. This was unusual as I got on fairly well with this fella who was a lot older than the rest of us. I probably should've taken a different angle. It was quite obvious that he was not in his right mind when he hurled 'slut' at me, but before we knew it a fist fight broke out, with me flinging a chair onto his head and back. The director of the school, who just happened to be passing through the studio at the time, witnessed the whole scene.

Later that week the fella approached me and apologised,

saying he had always felt that I was a sister to him and that he did not know what came over him. I felt that he was like a brother to me as well, but made it clear that if he ever spoke to me like that again he'd cop the same thing. He laughed and said, 'Yeah I know, sis.' We hugged and reverted straight back to a comfortable, fun relationship. It was as if the bad business between us had never happened.

The period from 1987 to 1990 was one of the best periods of my life, I reckon. Life overall had been good to me, albeit with the odd ups and downs, but there was something really special about the remaining four years I spent studying at Naisda. My physique began to improve dramatically, as did my strength and technique. I could literally feel and see my body transforming into what I was aiming for. It was empowering, exhilarating.

By the end of the second year, however, I noticed how immensely tired and thin I was becoming. It was getting to the point where I would just sleep all weekend. I had very little appetite, had become very weak and was beginning to look quite pale. Lenny's sister visited me one weekend and was shocked at the state I was in. She convinced me to go see a doctor. Somehow I had contracted hepatitis B. It was suggested that the constant close contact between dancers was most likely the cause. I was told to go back home to Naps and rest, as that there was nothing they could do. I returned home extremely weak and rake thin. I slept for the majority of that Christmas period and lived on porridge, only waking up to watch *The Bold and the Beautiful*. Big shame job, I know!

I had no plans to return to Naisda at the beginning of the following year. Physically I was in no state to. My condition had deteriorated badly and once more my aim of becoming a performer was threatened. However, Lenny unexpectedly turned up in Napranum and begged me to return. Somehow he convinced me and I commenced making last-minute preparations to continue into my third year. The long timeout back home and lots of prayer from Nan had taken effect. Even though I had physically deteriorated, I once more had the enthusiasm to tackle another year of physical challenges.

For the first couple of weeks back in Sydney I was required to live with the school's accountant Barbara and her daughter, as there was no room left at the hostel by the time I arrived. Another first-year student, Maroochy Barambah, was there as well. Maroochy and I connected in a unique way and to this day I maintain my friendship with her. Country and culture is at the core for us both.

Once rooms became available, several weeks into the course, we packed our bags and moved over to the hostel. On entering the room I was given, I realised the previous boarder had left some belongings behind. In the top drawer was a thin black jockstrap, plus a large amount of coins. In the drawer beneath were some ninja stars and a pair of nunchucks. On the back of the door was a poster of a majestic and dominating Bruce Lee with some fighting swords placed on either side of it. It wasn't half obvious what this person was into. I reported this to the office and later that evening opened the door to the deadliest looking fella making claim to the contents. His name was Danny Doyle and he was about to begin his first year of training. I made note of how interesting he looked and left it at that. I didn't think I'd have a chance with him, as I considered myself pretty plain in the looks department and thought that maybe his striking looks would've gone to his head, as happens with a lot of people in the dance world. Besides, I was with someone, even if it was an odd kind of relationship.

Throughout that year a slow shift occurred and I felt I was becoming more connected with the type of performer I was. My personal self or *voice* was beginning to make an appearance. I was extremely hungry for guidance and challenges from my teachers and trainers, but being the only female in the group I found I had to compete with the boys in my class for our principal choreographer's attention. He seemed to not be interested in what I had to offer. No matter how fast I learnt, no matter how dedicated and committed I was, his interest and focus stayed on the boys. He appeared to have no idea of how much I had respected his training and expertise. Mind you, sometimes he'd yell at us or throw his beloved clapsticks if we did not deliver according to his expectations, but I knew he was brilliant as an artist.

For the remainder of that year he continued to construct a piece for the boys as I sat patiently on the side, stretching and keeping my body and limbs warm in the hope that maybe I'd be called into the circle. He just didn't see me as part of his creativity. I soon realised that if I did not try to help I would look and feel embarrassed and unproductive when it came time for the end-of-year production. So with the help and guidance of Malcolm Sawyer, another teacher, I choreographed a piece for me to present at our end-of-year production titled *Innovations*. This piece was called *Woman Talk* and, I believe, sparked off the process of identifying and developing my personal choreographic voice. Inspired by my deep love for country, families and culture this piece was constructed using a bench as the only prop. A simple long black lace dress was offered to me as the costume. Within a week I had put *Woman Talk* together – some poetry I had written was pre-recorded to accompany the dance piece. The music evolved into a gospel song and concluded with pre-recorded harmonious singing by a chorus of Aboriginal women from Yirrikala, ending with the words 'don't take our Country, or we will die. How can you buy my grandfather?'

Following every performance of that piece the theatre was always dead silent, the only movement was my final rocking on that bench. I performed that piece every day for two weeks to an audience at Belvoir Street Theatre in Surry Hills with such immense pride, satisfaction and spirit. I realised that what I had gained from being ignored was worth so much more than parroting someone else's piece of work. At last I had found my performer's voice and could create accordingly.

CHAPTER SEVEN

My fourth year at Naisda, 1989, was a very exciting year indeed. Stephen Page, a former student who had gone on to study and travel with the Sydney Dance Company, returned to the school to direct the end-of-year production. Stephen brought back a lot of expertise and experience. Us students looked up to him and greatly admired what he had gone on to achieve with the highly successful, non-Indigenous, mainstream dance company. We were curious as to what he would have to offer to us; I know I definitely was.

By this stage, my on-again off-again boyfriend and I were sharing a two-bedroom apartment at Chippendale right next to The Block in Redfern. I really didn't know where I stood with him, as it was obvious we were drifting apart and had been spending less and less time together. One evening I decided to try to clarify things. He struggled with even speaking about the subject at first, but after much insisting that he be honest with me he came clean and blurted out that he did not love me. We had been together for two years, he had begged me to return to Naisda and even got the unit for us to move into, but all the while he didn't really feel for me the way I had thought he did. Although slightly confused and upset at first, and after much crying, I soon came around and thought fair enough.

I had been admiring that sexy fella who left his jockstrap in the drawer of my room anyway, so it was all good. Lenny and I left it at that but remained in the unit together, sharing the bills with another student who had also moved in with us. By now there were only three dancers left in our fourth year. We were close and worked reasonably well together. All of us knew that as fourth-year students we had to step up our physical abilities. This was not muck-around time. We had a certain standard to aspire to and it would've been a shame job if we couldn't achieve it, especially in terms of strength and technique. We didn't have to be perfect, but there were certain expectations. This was very difficult for us as dance students, as the majority of us had entered into the course without any prior training. Basically, we were all sculpted from scratch. When you consider that our five years of training began on an already developed body, the entry age having risen to eighteen, whereas the training of dancers in contemporary society often begins as early as three or five years old, then you can understand the pressure we were under to achieve and deliver in such little time. My observation was unless you worked your guts out for the short time you were in Naisda there was no way you would reach a reasonable standard by the time you graduated. You had to be hungry, disciplined, focus, consistent and systematic to achieve something by the end of it all.

My weaknesses were leg extensions, turns and lacking inner thigh strength, although there had been a dramatic improvement in my flexibility. My ex's turns were excellent and his physique and stamina were at a very good standard. The other student had also gained considerable strength by this stage, but there were times during his performance when he appeared as if he was on fast forward. He often seemed a little too revved up for comfort and always appeared to be dancing ahead of the music rather than with it. I really enjoyed the en masse rehearsals with all the different years assembled – when physiques that had been worked on all year had as little clothing on as possible and were covered in sweat. It was always a sight, especially some of those boy's midsections.

I really worked myself in terms of health, fitness and physique. All the focus, though, meant my mind was constantly processing. I began to find it difficult to sleep. At night I would walk from Chippendale through the city to Kings Cross where I would spend time at the Cosmopolitan Café, writing or just staring at the constant stream of people until the sun came up. Then I would walk back home, get dressed for school and track on into Glebe.

One particular morning I fronted up to the stairs outside our studio and there was Danny Doyle with his long black hair, wearing a long white coat sporting *Satan's worst nightmare* across the back of it, sipping a cup of coffee. My tummy did a somersault slightly as I became aware of the little crush I had for him. I decided to sit and make small talk as the doors hadn't been opened yet. It had been over a year since Danny had joined the school, but until then we had never really associated or spoken. He had a girlfriend and his own circle of friends and I just mainly did my own thing, not really socialising with anyone in particular. One time, however, when all the first-, second- and third-year students were about to board a travel coach and track it overland to the Northern Territory as part of their Remote Area Tour, everyone was busy hugging each other and somehow, even though we didn't really know each other, he came over and we hugged goodbye in a playful way. Anyway, after yarning a bit on the stairs it became obvious that we were both experiencing a mild case of insomnia. Something in common, I thought to myself.

In the days and weeks following we would find the time to have a quick yarn at the barre or in the hallway or student room downstairs, anywhere in fact. Danny would make comments that appeared to come from nowhere in particular. I found his interests to be slightly disconnected to reality. Regardless, I enjoyed the small talk, all the while admiring the sexiest hazel-coloured eyes peering out at me from behind his thick, almost blue-black hair. Danny wasn't like the other guys who seemed to be preoccupied with their looks and egos; he appeared oblivious to this. He really was his own person and not at all concerned with popular opinion. He seemed completely uninterested in impressing anyone whereas other students wanted to be noticed by the more popular teachers and choreographers and probably would have kissed butt if that's what it took. Not Danny. With him it was what you see is what you get, you either like it or lump it. He just existed in his own little bubble. His mannerisms also appeared to be a little offbeat as well – to say nothing of his wild beard.

Nevertheless, the more we yarned the more I found myself enjoying his company and the more I found myself fantasising about him. I mean, this guy would return to the hostel covered in sweat every evening, his sixpack glistening, much to the delight of myself and a few other girls who'd eye him off during his workouts in the lounge. Once, he arrived home from one of his jogging sessions, placed his feet on the sixth or seventh stair up and knuckles on the floor and proceeded to do push-ups. You should've heard the talk between us girls then!

That year was particularly exciting in terms of choreography, as well. One piece, *Dusk*, that Stephen Page had been experimenting with was to be showcased in the upcoming end-of-year production. I observed him intently; I studied his choreographic approach and technique closely. I saw the way he articulated his imagination through words and then demanded the physical body to enact what he wished to see manifest. I also observed his dynamic interactions with the students; one minute he was one of us, laughing, joking and having fun and then the next he became stern, distancing himself in order to focus on the bigger picture of what we were collectively working on. The process of experimenting with Stephen alongside the fifth-year students, as well as a handful of selected third-years, was something I treasured. The technique and the spirit behind it was something that I had not experienced previously at Naisda with any of the other choreographers. The majority of choreographers then were either African-American, non-Indigenous Australian or some other race, never our own – that is of Aboriginal or Torres Strait Islander background. Hence, the techniques and style carved into our choreographic voice and movement vocabulary were based on those of contemporary icons such as Twyla Tharp, Martha Graham and Lester Horton. This was the knowledge, expertise and experience that these non-Indigenous teachers brought with them and offered to us. But *Dusk* appeared to me to be a turning point, unique to this country alone. It had an energy that was ancient yet contemporary, it was fresh, dynamic and, well, us. Its style was animal mimicry in spirit, but created in a contemporary sense. I felt the ancient voice of my people close whenever I danced this piece. And I am not restricting my identity here to just Cape country, but, indeed, to this whole nation we know to be Australia. The music was constructed by Stephen's brother David Page and was deep, sensual and alluring, and reverberated throughout every cell in my body. The skin-tight unitard became one with my skin; I felt naked and free, metamorphosing from crocodile, to snake, to wallaby and to goanna in one long, slow motion.

For some reason, at one point, Stephen became frustrated with the piece and wanted to abandon it. I immediately thought no way, absolutely not. I was loving creatively growing from the exploration process too much to give up on it without a fight. I could sense a spirituality that was progressively manifesting before our very eyes. Somehow myself and another student convinced him to hang in there, arguing that if there was ever such a time for a piece like this to make an entrance it was then. That year a fresh new breed of Indigenous choreographers and dancers were beginning to emerge, experiment and break new ground. We were exploring something quite exciting – the likes of Marilyn Miller, Gary Lang and Bernadette Walong, to name a few, were of that generation. It was evident that it was time to construct movement through our own eyes rather than the African-American influence that had been dominating up until that point. Not that this influence was a bad thing, but it was obvious now our own ancient spirituality could manifest and take over. *Dusk* became the highlight of the end-of-year performance. I tasted the power and spirit of Aboriginal Australia every time I danced that piece. It was also recorded in a studio at the Opera House and was danced by Gary Lang, Russell Page, Lewis Lampton, Bernadette Walong and myself. This recording was aired as part of the ABC's *Black-out* series in 1989.

Like *Dusk*, *Munyahl Love* possessed that special ancient, sensual, almost erotic, magic. I absolutely loved dancing to it. The process of constructing this piece was similar to that of *Dusk* except this was a cluster of duets, a sensual piece where male and female chased and teased each other. It was erotic love-play in movement with ancient Indigenous sensuality in essence. To alternate between dancing with Lewis Lampton and Albert David was an absolute pleasure, throwing myself at them in artistic precision, creatively teasing, crawling, flirting, breathing in their physical energy and presence and knowing the entire time that I could re-enact this business story without any inhibitions whatsoever. I certainly wasn't complaining.

The lead-up to, and the performance of, our end-of-year production *Kayn Walu* was one of the most exciting creative processes I have experienced to date. The contemporary Indigenous fusion that manifested along with the ancient tribal spirituality of Yirrikala and Saibai Island traditional dances created a dynamic atmosphere that was simply awesome. I had also, by now, begun to write *Television Stories*, which Stephen choreographed. This piece explored the effects of domestic violence and alcohol abuse and attempted to highlight some of the issues that compound our people's lives. My written material was pre-recorded and I played the part of an abused person. One of our Yirrikala traditional tutors, Larry, also extended his role at the school and took to the stage in this piece, dramatically re-enacting a victim of substance abuse. It was all a definite boost to my self-esteem, especially considering I had long felt that writing would play a role in my own personal form of self-expression, whether on stage or in some other way.

That year I toured New South Wales and the Australian Capital Territory in collaboration with the fifth-year students who were my original group back in first year. I absolutely loved driving from place to place, sharing classes with other dancers, exchanging energies and, of course, performing.

A couple of hours before we were scheduled to present at the Canberra Civic Theatre, we were hanging out in our dressing room getting make-up and hair done when in walked several students from Naisda. They had decided to make the trip to support us during our performance, which was a part of the annual Floriade festival. You can imagine my delight when the last guy to walk into the room was none other than Danny Doyle. One of the other female dancers shot me a quick wink in the mirror and I quickly returned a small mischievous grin. Somehow word had gotten around that I had a thing for him. Would I have a chance with him that night? Following that performance we all decided to go clubbing. Danny and I spent most of the evening together, both on and off the dance floor, yarning, sharing drinks and carrying on. Before I knew it I had somehow taken him home with me. We had our first kiss outside the house where I was staying. There was something gentle about that kiss, yet it had a slow steady energy behind it. It was strong, but had a calming effect like a slow dance. As a consequence of the kiss passing the test I decided to let Danny stay the night. Before we knew it the following day had arrived and we were woken up by Danny's ride back to Sydney tooting the horn out the front.

'See ya back in Sydney then,' he whispered as he crawled out of bed, tying his hair into a ponytail and pulling his shirt over his head.

Oh . . . my . . . God! I thought to myself.

'Yeah see ya then,' I returned with a smile as I jumped out of bed and proceeded to walk him to the door and wave goodbye.

I had no idea what he thought of me and thought I'd just see what would happen on our return to school. Little did I realise what I was getting myself into.

CHAPTER EIGHT

I loved touring our country. Each year the school took the different levels to remote areas where we visited different communities for two to three weeks and learnt about the culture and traditions of those areas. Our destinations would alternate from a Torres Strait Island community to one on the mainland. What area we visited depended on our traditional tutors who spent some time with us each year at Naisda. If we had Saibai Island tutors then Saibai was where we visited; alternatively, if tutors were from somewhere in Western Australia then that would be the region we'd visit. During my time at Naisda I had the privilege of going to Western Australia, the Northern Territory and various islands in the Torres Strait, as well as New South Wales during my fourth and fifth years. The best thing about seeing country in this way is getting the opportunity to meet our people from other parts and taking the time to sit and listen and share our collective, yet distinct, identities with each other.

Our tour of Western Australia was absolutely awesome. I will never forget drifting off to sleep listening to the sound of singing and chanting by the respective custodians and then waking up to it as well. Apparently the people had sung in shifts to protect us from the spirits of the land, as we were of different *skin* to that country. The land was very unfamiliar to me – dry desert red dirt that stretched for miles, as far as the eye could see. Our accompanying tutors from that country would order the bus we'd be travelling in to stop if they saw a goanna or any other type of edible wildlife. As far as us students could tell, there wasn't anything out there, but sure enough one of the guides would exit the bus and walk straight to where the reptile would be hiding, start digging and pull it out by its tail. I remember jumping through the window and sprinting blindly across the dirt screaming in fear a large goanna when one of our guides flung one smack bang in the middle of the floor. There was no way I was going to share the ride with that thing, dead or alive.

During our time in Western Australia the locals promised to take us to a swimming hole. Imagine thirty or so crazy, urbanised young people all dressed up in their cut-off denim shorts and bikini tops complete with sunglasses, hats and sunscreen squinting into the distance wondering where the hell was this swimming hole that our tutors kept insisting was 'just up the road there'. Country went from absolutely nothing to a sudden huge drop right in front of us. Way down the bottom, crystal-blue water beckoned. Our tutors blessed us and introduced us to the spirits of ancestors in order to protect us and off we went. It was absolutely awesome.

I recall accompanying Ningali Lawford to visit her mum one time during that trip. Russell Page, the younger brother of

Stephen and David, was with me. The mum mistook us as being partners and after disappearing into the bedroom returned with a gorgeous huge *coolamun* – a utensil carved out of wood and used to carry things in.

'Here,' she said, holding it out toward us both. 'This is for you two.'

Russell immediately took ownership of that *coolamun* even though I would've wanted it.

'Thank you.' I graciously nodded.

Our trips up to the Torres Strait were just as rewarding, especially sitting with the elders. Sheer pride and joy manifested in the eyes and faces of our tutors when psyched-up students from the city poured into their usually quiet communities. We loved it when they arrived at our studio at Glebe, but it was something else to be with them on country itself. They so sincerely offered to us all they had – their songs, dances, cultural knowledge and families. It was one of the best things that Naisda had going, the fact that they made the effort to cultivate close relationships with traditional families from all over the country. This process kept us students spiritually fed as developing, evolving and maturing Indigenous artists, and was extremely important for us as it created a platform of awareness in terms of who we were and where we descended from; where we fit in contemporary Australia and, indeed, the rest of the world; and ultimately where it was we were going. Our elders taught the skills and techniques required to create any accompanying traditional costumes and props. And if singing was necessary then we'd also be introduced to the language as well.

As student performers we were required to present a performance at every community we visited. We quickly learnt to become flexible and adaptable no matter what situation we'd encounter. On one tour we had to assemble a stage floor from loose pieces of plywood so we could present our tap piece. Despite the fact that different sections kept coming apart mid-performance we hung in there and delivered, much to the delight of the locals in isolated areas such as Turkey Creek and Noonkanbah Station. How we didn't get caught between the sections is beyond me.

The same went for our visits to the islands. Modern and jazz pieces had to be done in the sand or dirt, as did partnering work. Changes would take place in makeshift dressing rooms erected from tarpaulins or hessian held up by poles and secured into the ground. I quickly learnt that in this industry there was little choice not to become embroiled with the other dancers. Gender etiquette really had no place unless it was specified by choreographers or when traditional protocol demanded it. Quick changes on the side stage meant that whoever was there would assist in undressing and dressing you. Any inhibitions we may have possessed about our bodies would have to be left at the door as two, or often three, pairs of hands endeavoured to dress a completely naked body in a matter of seconds. Likewise, on the floor bodies rolled on top of each other, intertwined in search of new ways of creating forms and shapes and movement. There was no time for shyness or being coy; my physical body was an instrument for creativity and expression first and foremost, any other usage of it became secondary. By fifth year it was nothing to strip down to our birthday suits and share showers or paint each other.

I remember the day us fourth and fifth years arrived back in Sydney upon completing our NSW tour. About an hour out some of us were getting quite excited. Two of the team had partners that they hadn't seen for five weeks and me, well, I didn't know what to expect with Danny. Would he have just continued with his on-again off-again relationship with his kind of girlfriend? Had he met someone else? Was I just some gammon girl he passed time with back in Canberra? I wasn't sure of anything, as no contact had been made since that night.

A couple of minutes away from the school there was a traffic jam. Three of us decided to jump out of the bus and run the rest of the way; we were obviously very eager to reconnect. I bolted up the stairs with one of the other guys and heard a commotion coming from Studio 1. It was Danny's group. He was unaware of the fact that we had arrived back and that two of us were sneaking a peek at their session. I just sat there trying to not making myself too visible so as to avoid distracting them. I watched him move and sweat and interact with the other students. I then saw him get quite close to the girl he was in an undefined relationship with and sort of playfully flick her hair from behind. The guy that I was sitting on the stairs with glanced at me. I quietly walked back down the stairs thinking that's that, he was still with her.

The following week, during morning class Danny kept coming up to me and attempting to make conversation. I ignored him, only giving short responses.

'Have I done something wrong?'

'Uhmm nah.'

'Well, it feels like I have.'

'That's too bad.' I kept stretching.

He remained quiet next to me, stretching.

'Uhm you better move away otherwise your woman might get jealous.'

'What woman?'

I nodded over to her.

'So this is what this is about, she not my woman.'

'I saw you flick her hair on Friday.'

'What? But youse weren't here Friday.'

'I was on the stairs watching youse rehearse. Youse didn't see us. I saw you go up to her and flick her hair.'

'I was just mucking around.'

'Yeah well it makes me uncomfortable after what happened between you and me in Canberra so can you just leave me please.'

'Hey I'll steer clear of her if that's what you want.'

'Yeah, we'll see,' I responded, as I kept stretching.

After that Danny began to make an effort with me, and we were soon spending more and more time together. He'd join me for lunch in the park or I'd invite him to accompany me on my weekend jaunts to Chinatown. One afternoon he invited me back to the place he was sharing with two of his friends in Norton Street, Leichhardt. Much to my delight he made damper and spaghetti bolognaise. I was very impressed. He had not struck me as someone who cooked. Before long we did everything together. He was very easy to talk to and appeared to have a thirst for life and interest in everything, particularly culture. He also had a sensitivity toward Christianity, which I respected. He was aware of my faith and beliefs as well as the fact that I was from community and had grown up with and among culture, so in a way we complemented each other. I began to really love his company and his attentiveness made me feel kind of special.

Church had always been a big part of my life, along with my faith and trust in God, although it often challenged me. Nan had always made sure I attended church.

'No matter we all different colour,' she would say, 'but we all have the same colour blood, and Jesus died for us all, not just whitefellas, or not just blackfellas, but us all. We all need him no matter how good we think we are, at the end of the day, we nothing without him.'

Nan's teachings regarding the importance of God, faith and Christianity were deeply embedded in me no matter how far I may have strayed, I always knew that much. I tried to find time to worship at the Christian Life Centre at Woolloomooloo in Sydney's inner eastern suburbs. I had been introduced to this church by my ex and found the fellowship was something I needed from time to time. I joined the church's creative team to have a creative outlet beyond the dance school environment and I felt that I was giving back to God what he had given to me: dance. There were six of us in the group who met weekly. Four were non-Indigenous dancers and then there was myself and my ex-boyfriend who was also still studying at Naisda.

One day when I was walking to church from Redfern, I could hear some loud talking up ahead. Immediately I knew that it was a group of my own mob, sitting around and most probably having a charge. As I got closer their faces lit up.

'Hey sister, sit with us, you wanna charge?'

'Na,' I responded, acknowledging them with a smile and nod as I kept walking.

'Aw come on now, don't be like that, come sit with us.'

'Nah gotta be somewhere, see yas,' I called back.

There was one female in this group. As I kept walking the woman decided to have her say.

'Hey what?'

Yep, I thought to myself, I was kind of expecting this. Here it comes.

'Ya think ya white or something? Think ya too good for us ay?'

I stopped dead in my tracks. I probably should've laughed it off and kept walking but no, I had to stop and respond. This kind of comment was the very kind of bullshit thinking that irked me about the mentality of some of our people – or anyone – equating being Aboriginal with being drunk in the gutter and having nothing better to do. It pushed the wrong button in me. I walked back to them.

'You know nothing about me.' I stood right in front of her.

'I know you think ya better than us, like ya white or something.'

'So you figure that I'm acting white cos I don't want to sit in that dirty gutter with you and drink, is that what ya saying?'

She didn't say anything.

'Me not wanting to drink with you doesn't make me think I'm white. It's sad you carrying on like this if you think that's what being black is.'

Silence.

'You don't know me or where I'm from,' I continued on, 'you should hold your tongue sister.'

She put her head down.

I walked off.

A couple of months into the relationship with Danny I sensed that we were a mismatch of sorts. He was fun and sexy and polite, but there was something about his mannerisms that I couldn't quite click with. I addressed this sense of uncertainty on my part by attempting to break it off with him before we progressed any further. I had noticed how expressive he had been with a couple of other girls at the dance school as well and this bothered me. Deep down I felt that something was missing, just wasn't quite right.

We were walking through Redfern on our way to the unit I shared with my ex when I tried to explain why I thought we should stop seeing each other.

'Did you hear what I said?' I asked.

'This always happens to me,' Danny responded.

'What do you mean? I don't understand what you're saying?'

'This, this breaking up. This always happens.'

I really didn't understand what he meant.

'Something doesn't feel right. I don't think you and I are right for each other,' I continued.

We walked the rest of the way to the unit in silence. On our arrival at the unit Danny kept walking down the street. I let him go, thinking that was that. Nan and my sisters were visiting that year and staying at the unit with us. About half an hour later my sisters came into my room, all excited, sporting a single red rose and a Cherry Ripe chocolate bar. Danny had apparently returned and left the offering for me.

'Don't Fay sorrrrry one, poor fella,' sooked Barbara, pulling a face that spelled sorrow and compassion for this fella who she didn't really know anything about.

I didn't really know him either for that matter, well, apart from what I had experienced to date. But for some reason I was out the door and calling to him to return. From that day on we remained committed to each other.

About four months into the relationship, toward the end of 1989, we were sitting in the park having lunch when, amid mouthfuls of a hamburger, Danny blurted out, 'Let's go get a ring ay?'

'Uhm, yeah ok.' I shrugged.

Not the most romantic setting. What was I thinking? Each of us must've needed that something that the other provided. We were both so young and should've been focusing on our careers, and we barely knew each other, but we hadn't done the usual 'let's get to know each other first' and trial a relationship. To continue on now with a trial didn't even cross my mind. Comments were made about how fast things were progressing between us, that I didn't know what I was doing, that it would affect me for the rest of my life, but I took no notice. We were like chalk and cheese in a way, there was no doubt about that. Was it the lust, the company, the security of companionship in a city where no family was around? Was it all the nice little things he kept doing for me that made me feel so special in a way that I had never felt before? Or was it the fact that I thought he was just the most gorgeous Murri fella ever?

Whatever it was, I did not think twice about what I was getting myself into. I'd had dreams prior to getting married. I knew I wanted to make it, whatever 'it' was – a dancer, actor, teacher, writer – and to travel overseas. I was about to taste at least one of my dreams. I had been training in dance for the past four years and even though it was bloody hard work I knew I was getting there. A career as a performer now began to appear very likely. During the course, my interest in acting began to unfold and I could feel myself getting hungry for more. I had seriously been considering the National Institute for Dramatic Art (NIDA) and spoke with our course coordinator about the possibility of auditioning. I did not for one second think that my relationship with dance and performance would be affected as a result of marrying Danny. I didn't know if he loved me, really loved me. Hell, I didn't even know what love was. I still don't think I know. All I knew was that he had made it clear that he wanted to be with me. I was too young and blind for intelligent thinking, so I just went with the flow of things.

We set 13 January of the following year as our wedding day and, after informing the rest of the school of our decision, proceeded to make the necessary arrangements.

'Trust you to choose the thirteenth,' giggled his ex-girlfriend when he told her the news. 'You know the number thirteen is bad luck hey?'

The ceremony was held at the Christian Life Centre, followed by photos at Centennial Park and the reception at the dance studio back in Glebe. Nan and Mum were able to attend and fortunately for us they were able to stay with an old friend who was a nurse at Napranum when I was a teenager. I just informed Nan and Mum that I was getting married – I did not seek their permission. Nor did they try to stop me. They just accepted it was my decision and made preparations to at least be there for me. I vaguely recall one of my family members asking if Danny was 'community' or 'city'. I informed him that he was 'city fella' but that he respected culture, and that was that. I wished my sisters could've been there on the day as well, but Sydney was such a long way from Napranum and there was no way everyone could've made it. I've often wondered how Mum and Nan really felt about my decision to marry at such a young age and at the most crucial stage of my career, but at no point did they discuss what I was about to do. Most of Danny's siblings, some of his nephews and his mother attended the wedding. I had not met any of them previously and had no idea what they were like. Nor did they know anything about me.

A lot of the students and some of the teachers were slightly confused as to our quick marriage and doubted whether it would last. Having said that, students, teachers and friends alike rallied together and supported us. Sisters Delores and Jules Scott provided my flowers. Amanda Snee (aka Tunstall) and her boyfriend provided the vehicles and hotel on our wedding night. Sidney Saltner did all the cooking and made the wedding cake and decorated the icing in earthy colours. The school's seamstress, Melody, made our wedding outfits, which Dan and I designed. Others contributed in many different ways, taking care of so many things I would've otherwise overlooked. I was so grateful for everyone's support. I knew nothing about what needed to be done; all I knew was that I wanted to 'do the right thing' and be with Danny.

We had our reception in Studio 1 at the dance school. Dan and I went barefoot, as we'd run out of dollars before we knew it. My budget went on purchasing shoes for my bridesmaid Tracey, a fellow student and housemate. Danny's brother Lionel was best man. Our wedding tune was the sound of the didgeridoo played as I made my way down the aisle locked arm in arm with my modern dance teacher and dad for the day, Ronnie Arnold. After less than half a year together and just two weeks after my twenty-first birthday and neither with nor without the blessings or approval of Mum or Nan, I gave up my own name and became Danny Doyle's wife.

CHAPTER NINE

Being married and continuing on as a student did feel odd to me. I didn't see myself in the same way as I had prior to getting married. I was now someone's wife and not my own person. I could not do what I wanted, whenever I wanted. I had someone else to consider. I did not regret the decision we had made but just felt different. Regardless, I commenced my fifth and final year as best I could. The worst thing was separating physically from Danny every day, as we had become inseparable. My body was no longer only set aside for dancing and meeting the demands of the course; it was now connected to Danny and it didn't take too long before it all began to take its toll on me physically. All I wanted to do in the mornings was stay cuddled up in bed beside him and sleep all day, rising only for a feed or to go to the movies or the beach. The last thing I wanted to do was dance for eight hours every day, five days a week. I had obviously become spoilt in a really short space of time.

Danny had decided to quit the course several months after our wedding to take up photography while I focused on getting my head around my new life and pulling myself together. We agreed that being around each other twenty-four seven was probably not for the best. And being in an environment as full-on as Naisda as a young married couple was probably not the best way to kick things off either. With Danny gone from the dance school I felt that I could at least breathe a little and have some focus reserved for class and its demands.

My group kicked off that year with another tour of New South Wales, this time joining forces with two students from fourth year. These two were quite advanced in their technical ability; especially the girl who was the most focused one out of the entire school, I reckon. As much as I loved touring and performing I began to suffer separation anxiety. Danny made the effort to break the length of time we were apart and visited us in Newcastle. However, I began to sense our course coordinator may not have approved. Certainly Danny's arrival caused me to fall back into just wanting to be with him. It got in the way of my focus and discipline.

Following that three-week tour we were scheduled to fly to Hong Kong on our first overseas trip and then continue on with another three weeks in the Northern Territory. I knew I couldn't do another five weeks of touring and we were only halfway through the first leg. I did not have the drive, strength and focus necessary to deliver professionally. I had to make a decision. Of course I wanted to do the Hong Kong tour; one of my dreams was to travel overseas and perform. It was just weeks away. I couldn't believe it. I was so excited. But I spoke to the course coordinator about my situation and told her that even though I would be able to do Hong Kong I had decided that I needed timeout and that I would not be able to do the Northern Territory tour afterwards. The coordinator appeared to accept what I said and gave me the impression that it was all fine with her, that I would be able to take timeout as proposed. Little did I know that she was being dishonest and had no intentions of keeping me as part of the Hong Kong tour group. If she had given me an ultimatum straight-up then of course I would have chosen to hang in there and do all three tours, but because she appeared to have accepted what I told her I assumed all would be well and that I would just reconnect with the group following the final leg. But this was not the case at all.

In the week leading up to our intended departure date, I arrived at school excited and pumped. On entering the office area I immediately learnt that my group had gone ahead without me to make final preparations before travel. I thought it was odd that they did not wait for me, but, regardless, I thought maybe I had just got the times wrong, that there would be an explanation. I went over to the course coordinator who, appearing immediately cold and stand-offish, directed me into the music room. Her body language and tone were different to her usual self. Shortly afterwards the artistic director of the school joined us. I had no idea what they were about to dish out to me. I thought that worst case scenario I'd get a lecture for my decision to have timeout during a tour. I was wrong. They proceeded to tell me that I had been dropped from the Hong Kong tour and only then did they say that if I had wanted to do the tour I needed to do the extra three weeks on our arrival back in Australia.

Looking back now I should've just taken a deep breath and complied, but instead I sat there and began to argue the point. To cut a long story short, I told them to shove the trip and that I would not be bribed or treated in this way. I continued to rant on about how I was going to get overseas one day and I wouldn't have to trade my pride for a gammon lollipop dangled in front of me by some gammon dishonest people. With that I ran out of the office and through Studio 2 downstairs. By this stage members of the tour group had returned. I felt so betrayed by them. I thought that they would've at least stood up for me or something. I guess that was my first real experience of the dog-eat-dog culture of the industry. My heart was upset and my head was spinning. I don't even know why I reacted in such a way or why I had been so dramatic. I ran out of the building and onto the road as traffic skidded to a halt, drivers tooting angrily at me. I just plonked myself right there in the middle of Glebe Point Road and practically sobbed my heart out. A nun walking past ventured out onto the road toward me and after some time consoling me managed to lead me back onto the footpath. I remember Lenny, my ex, on one side of me and Danny, who must've either come in with me that day or had responded to a phone call and raced over to Glebe from Redfern, on my other side. They both just sat there for as long as it took for me to get the frustration, pain and anger out. It must've been an hour by the time I appeared over it and ready to move on.

'Wanna go shoppin', babe?' Danny gently whispered to me.

Through sniffles I nodded as he took my hand and we made our way toward the bus-stop. I hugged my ex before he turned and walked back into the dance school.

The day my group flew out I stayed in bed all day and cried with Danny beside me waiting on my every need and request.

While they were away in Hong Kong experiencing what I had always wanted to do I felt like I was just not a part of the team, that I had been betrayed by all of them. I wondered why my two immediate group members had not stuck up for me. I know I would've fought for them had it been them in my shoes. I did not understand how you could work as part of a group in such a close environment, pouring your guts out, sweating every day and then treat someone like that. I could not trust them and so could no longer be part of the group. Regardless of it being my last year I just dropped out. I didn't care about graduating after that.

'Let's just leave,' suggested Danny.

'Hey? What? To where?'

'Let's go to Napranum,' he suggested.

'To live?'

'Why not?'

'What about your photography?'

'Eh, it's only a course. I know enough about that stuff anyway,' was his reply.

I was too empty to even think about what he was suggesting. I just went with the flow. Danny and I packed up our stuff from the two bedroom unit we had at Dulwich Hill and moved to Napranum. Danny had always said that he wanted to experience life in a community.

I ached for dance every day after moving back to Napranum. Danny got work with the council while I just spent time with Nan whenever she had time to spend with me. I realised there was still so much more to learn about culture. Culture is not a course, being Indigenous isn't learnt, it's *being*. Just as I observed her as a child when out on country, I had the opportunity once more to continue on with this learning cycle, except this time I was a young woman. I found myself back in the bush looking for yams, trudging through the mangroves collecting *ndrangle*, or pulling crab out of the mud or collecting *chaay* or acool shells, as they are more commonly known. I was living a cultural lifestyle once more as I had done during my childhood. Once more I witnessed Nan talking to old people: '*Coooow*' she would call out when we would enter deep scrub. '*Nung lin* ooohhhh, *nan njumam mundri*, we your people. *Iyoncha lin. Nung caķ nyar ah iyee nan chee*.' She would address the spirits and inform them of who we were, that we were present on country and what we required from the land. I took all this in from a different perspective this time around. I also spent a lot of that year documenting the stories that she had told me and continued to share with me.

I knew, though, that I had to return back to Naisda to finish my fifth and final year, so about six weeks before the annual end-of-year production I rang and asked if I could be a part of it. To my surprise there were no problems, it was almost as if they were waiting for my call. There were absolutely no issues concerning my travel or re-entry, although I was later told that one student had been going around the school with the intent of acquiring signatures to prevent me coming back into the school. Before I knew it I was back in training, I quickly learnt the necessary choreography. My ex kindly allowed me to stay with him during that time. Then one day during rehearsal I was told that there was a phone call for me in the office.

'Hello.'

'Babe, come and open the door for me.'

'Hey? Where are you?' I asked, confused.

'I'm here, in Sydney. Arrived this morning. I'm at Lenny's place.'

'I'll be there soon,' I informed him.

Dan ended up getting a hotel room for us for the remaining month just around the corner from Oxford Street.

My final performance at Naisda, *Djumba Woman* directed by Raymond Blanco, was a real cultural experience working with traditional elders from Turkey Creek. One of the dances they taught us was so strong culturally that I ended up getting sick and one of the female elders had to blow and put smell on me. In fact, two of us students were affected spiritually by the traditional dances that year; the other student was Christine Anu, who has since gone on to become one of this country's most celebrated Indigenous singers.

On finale night all I could think was I did it! It had been a long hard slog, but at twenty-one I had completed the course. I was grateful for every single experience I encountered throughout that time. I was grateful for Nan's constant visits year after year supporting me through it all. Nan would've attended several end-of-year shows by the time I finished. How she managed to I'm not sure now. Sadly Mum never got the chance to see me perform at all. I wish she had, but, without fail, Nan would appear in the audience year after year unannounced, her strong, stern face prominent amid the audience. 'Oh my God, who's that deadly black woman in the audience? She scares me,' was a comment all too commonly made by students who didn't realise that this was my nan. Her presence would inject strength in me to perform my best. Her support and pride in what I was doing was obvious.

Throughout my time at Naisda I had begun to see my country, my people and our culture through very different eyes. I appreciated and valued what we collectively had as a nation and as First Nations people more than I ever had before. Following the *Djumba Woman* production a new phase back on country awaited us. My plan to audition for NIDA, although remaining in my heart, was pushed to the back of my head never to be followed through. I don't know why I did not pursue it then or even later on throughout my twenties, but, regretfully, I just didn't. For the second time Dan and I boarded the plane. As we tracked our way back to the Cape I had a strange sense that I was leaving someone very special behind although I didn't know who for sure.

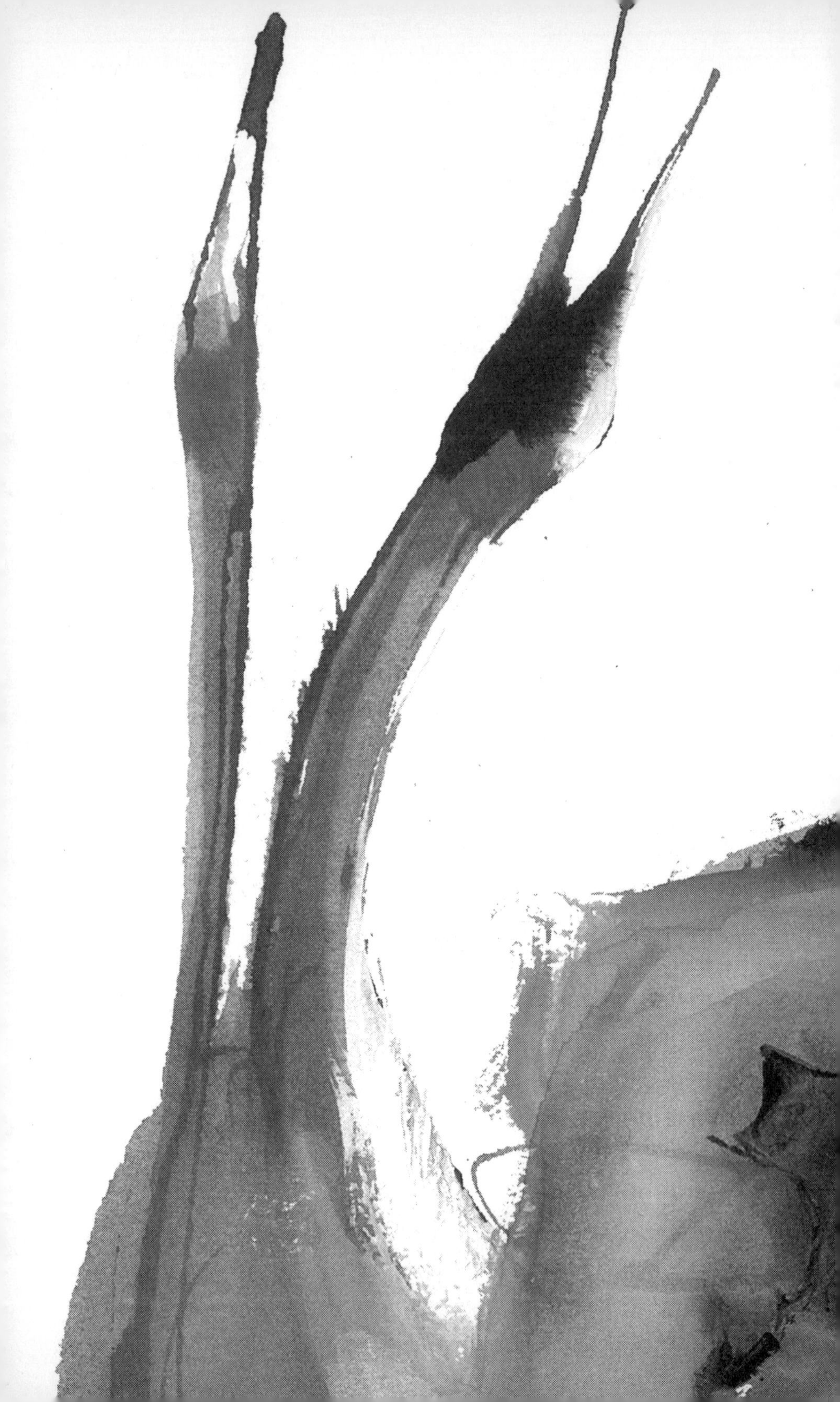

part 2

Growing Into Self

CHAPTER TEN

What was I doing back in Napranum? Somehow the wind had carried me back there. Dan and I moved back into 1 Peppan Street with Nan and all of a sudden I went from not having family near me at all for years to suddenly being surrounded by them all day every day. It was pretty full-on. At a time when I should've been searching out other avenues for furthering my career in the arts or auditioning for NIDA, here I was back where I had started. This time, however, I did have years of experience living in Australia's largest city under my belt, as well as exposure to the rest of the country and a qualification. If I look at it from that angle, I wasn't doing too bad.

Danny got work with the council again in various locations around the community while I dabbled in the position of editor of the local community paper *Napranum Cha*. I enjoyed this experience and received a lot of support not only from personnel at the training centre, but also from the then editor of the local *Weipa*

Bulletin. What kept me creatively focused was a promise made by the council to build a performance and training venue that Dan and I would manage. This building was to be erected on the grounds where the old church once stood in the old mission area. Measurements were taken and a design of the overall layout was made available for us to view, discuss and approve. It had been demonstrated to us, in that first year back home, that we would be able to contribute creatively back into the community in the area of performing arts. For some reason it never came to pass, and no report or explanation was even provided to us.

As Dan and I progressed into our second year of marriage life pretty much carried on the same. We became more engrossed in local community affairs and business. Every now and then I would contemplate our love for each other. It always felt to me that something was missing between us. Doubt was constant but I always pushed it way down inside of me so it wouldn't affect me.

Around the middle of 1991 bruises started to appear on my body. I had no idea what was causing them and pretty much just ignored them. As the weeks progressed the bruises started to get bigger in size and much brighter in colour. People probably suspected that things weren't quite so smooth between Dan and me but no-one actually said anything. When my gums started bleeding for no apparent reason I decided to take myself up to the local clinic. I got a double dose in the news department that morning. Not only was I three months pregnant, but I had also developed a condition known as idiopathic thrombocytopenia purpura, or ITP, which basically means my immune system turned on itself and my antibodies were gobbling up my platelets. There was no explanation for why all of a sudden this had happened, though the pregnancy may have had something to do with it. The lowest average platelet count in a normal healthy person is around 150,000. I was walking around basically a dead woman at a count of 20,000.

Before I knew it I was flown out to Cairns Base Hospital, hooked up to a machine, practically wrapped in cotton wool and treated as if my life was almost over. The slightest bump or cut would have me literally bleeding to death. I kept asking about the baby. Was the baby safe? Were the steroids they were about to start pumping into me going to affect the baby in any way? Each time the response was a firm and direct: 'Miss, as far as we are concerned there is no baby. You are our focus. If you get through this then there will be a baby to focus on. This is not about the baby at this stage, this is about you.'

The whole process was a bit of a wait. They moved me from the open-air shared space in the hospital and gave me my own room for privacy. Out the window I had full view of the comings and goings at a gymnasium. Being confronted with this visual every day had the potential to depress me by reminding me I was unable to do what these people were able to do with their lives. I endured the 'why me' sook stage in the early days. But then I realised what I was going through was not necessarily a death sentence, regardless of what I overheard a couple of nurses, who thought I was asleep, say about my situation one day.

'It's a wonder this one is still doing okay.'

'Why is that?'

'We had an older guy and a younger boy of about ten in with the same condition recently and neither made it. Here we have an Indigenous woman carrying a child. We don't really know how this will turn out or better still if she'll respond to the treatment effectively.'

I stirred a bit so they would shut up with that kind of talk. I did not want to hear any more of it. I recalled the experience with the song marble at twelve and the contracting of hepatitis B at nineteen and thought no way, God is not going to bring me this far, blow a baby in my belly just for me to cark it two years into my marriage. I shifted the focus of my heart, mind and spirit onto healing and getting on with my life. I knew I was going to walk out of there okay and holding that baby in my arms.

In the meantime Danny had given up his work and travelled down to Cairns overland in the first vehicle we had purchased, a seventies model Toyota LandCruiser trayback. He brought down with him a pretty-faced wallaby that we had inherited after one of his numerous hunting trips out bush. We called it Legs as it appeared to have more legs than anything. I recall being heavily sedated on pethidine – something I became extremely fond of while in hospital – watching the doctor dance around me when in walked Danny with his shoulder bag sporting the Aboriginal flag on it. Suddenly out popped this little wallaby. Dan had brought Legs right into the operating room.

I was required to remain in hospital to get my platelet count up to a reasonable 40,000 and then continue to visit the hospital every day for intravenous dosages of immunoglobulin. We achieved 70,000 just before the seven-month mark. Once more I questioned the doctor.

'What about my baby?'

'What do you mean?'

'I've taken a lot of drugs for the majority of the time I've been pregnant. Will my baby be affected in any way?'

'As mentioned earlier, worst case scenario, the baby may not survive. However, if the baby does, there is the possibility that he or she may inherit some features that could be the result of the drugs you've been administered.'

'Features like what? Will it be deformed?'

'No, not deformed but the features may be, let's say . . . prominent, in some way.'

I gave him a confused look. 'What do you mean?'

'The features could be somewhat sharp in appearance.'

What the hell? I really couldn't make sense of what he said. There was one thing that I did know for sure though and that was that I was going to ignore it. My baby would be born alive, healthy and absolutely gorgeous.

At around nine-thirty on the morning of 6 March 1992 at the Cairns Base Hospital, and after a six-hour labour without any drugs and with Danny eating a meat pie while staring sleepily up the passageway our baby was about to journey down, I decided to jump off the bed and squat onto a mirror in preparation to push and then pull out from inside of me Sheridan Nyrlotte. My platelet count was averaging between 70,000 and 90,000. It was enough to consider me safe. I knew it was almost time to push when I recalled the advice my friend Stef Furlong gave me: 'Fay, you will feel like a big watermelon is trying to make its way out of your bum. When you feel this, then it's time to push.'

Before I knew it the baby was out and cradled in my arms. She was warm and this was truly a most incredible, amazing experience. *Nyrlotte* means rare white waterlily and was the name of my maternal great-grandmother. It was chosen by Nan even before we knew I was carrying a girl. We immediately checked her face and counted everything. It was all there and apart from looking like a squashed up little pink-faced wallaby she seemed pretty normal. Immediately the hospital tag sporting 'Doyle baby' went on her wrist. We didn't want to risk losing her to the white mums in the hospital. She had appeared to be a little on the milky side.

Later on that day I held this pink little thing in my arms waiting for a bed to become available. I couldn't believe I had brought this little person into the world and that she was mine. I just kept staring at her. Slowly she began to open her eyes. It took a while but once her eyelids finally stabilised we just stared at each other.

'Hello bubba,' was all I could manage.

Sheridan just kept staring at me. She had the most beautiful blue eyes. For the first time in a long time I wondered about my biological father again. There was no way he could know that he now had a granddaughter as well as a daughter. Does my existence ever cross his mind like his does mine? I wondered.

Dan and I settled back into constructing some sort of life in Napranum with Sheridan. Prior to our return to Naps we had traded the Toyota for a smaller car so we could put a baby capsule in the back. Sheridan was a very demanding baby and nothing in the world could have prepared me for her presence. Suddenly I felt like my life was owned by this screaming infant. I existed for her demands alone. She was an absolute angel as long as I was within sight responding to her every beck and call. But the minute she couldn't see me it was on. She demanded around-the-clock attention and it drove me nuts. This child resembled an angel, yet in spirit she was as wild and fiery as both her great-grandmother and her namesake old Nyrlotte, her cousin, or in whitefella kinship terms her great-great grandmother.

By this stage Nan had requested that downstairs be built into a granny flat to accommodate her while Danny and I took over upstairs. We also got the veranda built in to provide an extra room. Lynette and Bobby lived at the back of us at Kwokkanum Street, on the land where Nan and Grandad once lived. Mum and my other sisters still remained at Callope Street.

During Sheridan's first year Danny and I continued an association with the arts the best way we could considering our isolated location. The schools kept us contributing creatively as choreographers, workshoppers and guest performers. This challenged me to work toward transforming the baby figure I had acquired as a result of my pregnancy and bounce back to my former shape and fitness ability. I wasn't in the mainstream dancing professionally, but still resembling a dancer and delivering as effectively as possible was important to me. When Sheridan was just three months old Dan and I were back on stage performing at Weipa's first theatre restaurant at the Albatross Hotel. Danny told me that the manager was interested in us putting on a performance to entertain people as they dined. I got straight back into choreographic mode and began a forty-minute segment. There were a couple of dance duets by Danny and myself, as well as solos. It seemed as if Dan was happy to hand over the creative component to me. He never fought me on anything, just supported. We complemented each other in that respect. We were very fortunate to have some big song-and-dance elders contribute to the traditional component of the show as well. These four siblings were my three grandfathers and one grandmother of the Apalich, elders to me through my great-grandmother Nyrlotte. It was such an honour. During this period we made the most of just sitting around the fire and listening to these four tell stories. Well, only three of them told stories. The older sibling did not really care much for talking. All he did was sing for ceremony, an honour indeed.

We lasted approximately two years in Napranum with about three months of that spent in Aurukun. Danny had been offered a job as a youth and recreation officer there so off we went. I thought it would be a good time to reconnect with families there and Danny was also extremely interested in learning more about culture. He was kept busy working towards upgrading the sport and recreation facilities and having programs available for the youth and sport-orientated, while I remained at home caring for Sheridan and continued to network with families, particularly those rich in cultural knowledge. Visits from Granny Annie, one of the Yunkaporta siblings and big song woman, along with her daughter and my Aunty Gladys Tybingoompa were daily occurrences. Never before had our little voice recorder come in so handy. I recorded songs and storytelling around the clock. These two grannies yarned to me the story of *Woonk*, a legend consisting of song, dance and story that begins at Coen and travels all along Wik country. This story is huge and I interpret it as an Indigenous version of *Romeo and Juliet*. One of the lovers ends up drowning themselves in a lagoon or swamp as a result of a broken heart. A whirlpool can still be seen in the area. Nan visited Aurukun regularly too. This was a far cry from the life I left behind in Sydney. I basically went from constant dance classes, workout sessions and partying to nursing a baby and listening to ceremonial singing and stories from grannies. These two grandmothers of mine shared so much with me during this time. Sheridan would be asleep either on Nan's lap or on a blanket in the centre of us three women. I can recall the tempo and rhythm of their voices in a split second.

The place where we lived in Aurukun was haunted. There was absolutely no doubt about it, I reckon. I felt a spirit presence watching my every move, so much so that I refused to leave Sheridan alone in her room, which the spirit inhabited. The more I felt it, the more concerned I became for Sheridan. This spirit had a heavy energy about it. It was either a dark spirit or something bad had happened in that room and I did not want my baby's first year in a place that held such energy.

It was obvious that Danny was really enjoying his time in Aurukun, but I wasn't prepared to remain there for much longer. For a start I was fast getting over the expensive charter flights we had to keep paying for if we wanted to make a quick trip to Weipa to shop for groceries. I never really did enjoy small three-seater planes, particularly since the time Danny and I flew in one from Cairns to Weipa earlier on in our marriage. Regardless of the fact that there was a cyclone hovering around the far north I had to make that trip. *Cogai* Myrtle Chevathen had passed away. She had spoiled me when I was younger, constantly giving me money whenever I visited Aurukun or she Weipa. I was considered one of her favourites, so had to attend the funeral. That day the commercial flights north were all cancelled and the only way I could get home in time was on a chartered plane. There was Dan and myself in the back as well as a young female teacher on her way to Horn Island in the Torres Strait. We must've been up in the air about thirty minutes or so when the plane really started to shake. The further we went the worse it got. No-one spoke. At its worse point I noticed the pilot struggling to keep his hands on the wheel. He turned around and looked at Dan and I with a hopeless look on his face. By this stage the woman up the front was throwing up, with fear I suppose.

'This is it babe, we're going down in a cyclone,' Dan blurted out, laughing. He placed his arms around me, drawing me closer. I put my head down on his lap and shut my eyes. What a thing to say to your new wife! Anyway, before I knew it we had flown past Weipa and the pilot informed us that it was safer to head straight for Horn Island. Apparently he had flown on top of the winds. Landing on ground never felt so good. We were able to stretch our legs, breathe and kiss the earth, but I knew it wasn't over. The pilot convinced us to continue back to Weipa, saying that we would be fine if he flew low the whole way. I knew families were waiting on me before they could proceed with the funeral, so I decided to trust the pilot and God, of course.

As part of his job, Dan had to plan and accompany Aurukun's representatives to both the Laura Dance Festival and the region's football carnival, which hosted teams from all over the Cape. The Aurukun teams were successful on both trips, but Danny returned back from the Kowanyama trip sporting the ugliest form of gravel rash on one of his bum cheeks. It was massive and no amount of antibiotics could relieve him from the pain and discomfort. Eventually he turned to the bush medicine that Nan had taught him and within days of applying it to the infected area it was completely healed. The recovery time was amazingly fast. Nan had always sworn by this particular medicine, but I had never seen it work in quite the same way as it did for Danny that time.

After about three months I informed Dan that I believed a bad spirit inhabited the place we were living in and just like that he put his notice in and back to Weipa we went. We hadn't even been in Aurukun that long. But a house was waiting for us and Danny getting another job would be no problem. Besides, Nan would be happy to have us back home.

CHAPTER ELEVEN

When Sheridan was about two the travel bug hit us again. I was getting bored with the lifestyle in Weipa and I think Dan was too. I loved the simplicity of it all, but sometimes it got a little too slow for my liking. As a twenty-four-year-old young mum, I had decades of creative energy just sitting inside me and there was no way I was ready to live life at that pace. We packed our stuff and moved to Brisbane.

Our time in Brisbane lasted only a couple of years and consisted mainly of attempting to survive. We had been boarding at Dan's brother's place along with his wife and little son, who was about a year older than Sheridan. By this stage both Dan's brother's family and us were full-on in the Christian movement and the time we spent together had been fulfilling and fun, but it was inevitable that we'd eventually get in each other's way, which is exactly what happened. However, it challenged us to let go of the security and comfortable familiarity of family and move on.

The struggle we had as a young family with no real financial security in a large city scared the crap out of me. I could not believe we weren't financially stable by that stage. I began to really miss the support we had had back home. Perhaps we'd made a mistake by moving to Brisbane. Following several depressing months in a small two-bedroom flat at Kangaroo Point, a two-storey townhouse was offered to us in East Brisbane and eventually Danny landed a job as a security guard at South Bank. I breathed a sigh of relief as our savings were almost depleted by that stage. We now had a decent enough place along with a regular income coming in. Sheridan was enrolled in kindergarten next to the Woolloongabba stadium and soon a routine was established for the three of us. We did not have a car, so I'd walk everywhere and push Sheridan in a stroller.

A while later, Danny decided to go on a Christian camp somewhere on the coast up north leaving Sheridan and myself behind. One afternoon, I was sitting in the lounge while Sheridan played in front of the television when I noticed this whitefella who kept passing the front of our place, constantly looking in. At one point he actually looked directly at me and we maintained eye contact for several seconds before I got up and shut the curtains. I didn't think much of it but that fella had given me the creeps with his blatant prying into our space.

That night, after I put Sheridan to bed, I was settling into a book when I got this strong sense of needing to pray for protection. No matter how much I tried to ignore it, the feeling would not go away. Eventually I succumbed. After the prayer I decided to just lay there. I had no sooner shut my eyes when almost immediately I had a vision of being raped. At that point I also heard a bang downstairs. Immediately a voice in my belly instructed me to go to the toilet that was across the hall from my room, even though I had no need to go. I listened. The next directive was walk softly so I would not be heard and to not turn the lights on in the bathroom. Then to just sit on the toilet being as quiet as possible. I heard a loud thud, this time coming from directly underneath the bathroom and again I was instructed to not turn the tap on. I was then told to quietly exit the bathroom and stand at the top of the stairs. I could just see the outline of a person at the bottom. As I moved slightly to get a better focus the figure stood still. By this stage I'd realised there was another figure already halfway up the stairs. This person was tall and seemed to have quite broad shoulders.

Once I realised that there were two people in the house my whole body went completely numb. A couple of seconds passed before I whispered, 'Who's there?' Both people just stood still. Next thing, I ran down stairs screaming, 'get . . . out . . . of . . . my . . . house'. The two figures bolted out the kitchen door and then out the gate into an alleyway. I then realised that the bangs I had heard were them removing the kitchen window. I grabbed the biggest knife I could find and rang Dan's sister, who then rang the brother we'd previously lived with, as he was just down the road. At that point in our lives we really didn't have anything worth stealing and I had a strong feeling that these guys were after my precious girl and me. I shudder to think what would've happened if I hadn't listened to that voice in my belly and am now convinced that I had God's protection that night.

Even though the townhouse was good quality considering the affordable rent, our neighbours on either side were somewhat 'challenging'. On our left was a single mum who worked as a stripper and the type of people who frequented her place had me concerned for Sheridan. The neighbours to our right fought constantly. The screaming, name-calling and violent crashes that penetrated the common walls became too much after a while. I did not want my girl growing up in this way. She already had trouble mixing in with the children of the block. For some reason they wouldn't play with her and treated her differently. I could tell she was lonely and needed friends.

I left the possibility of conceiving again open and within months I saw a visual of a cashew-shaped image deep in my woman area. I knew immediately what this meant. Financially we were nowhere near secure, but my cultural upbringing dominated and allowed me to accept it. A pregnancy test confirmed I was nine weeks pregnant. As usual, Danny just accepted the news. He took into consideration the fact that I had never really gotten over the break-in and had never felt safe after it. The incident really shook me. I had full-on experience living on the community with bloodshed, physical violence and spiritual encounters, but this was not the same. As a result of it all, Danny put his notice in and bought a green Toyota Tercel. We packed it with whatever little possessions we had and kicked off for Cairns.

Dan worked as a security guard and occasional performer while I grew into a whale. I watched Danny rehearse and prepare for performance and then would stare at my ever-growing stomach in the mirror. Gone was my deadly dancer physique and here was Danny looking deadlier than ever and around other dancers with tight bodies. My only contact with the arts was choreographing for Danny as well as observing performances so I could offer feedback, and even then I felt uncomfortable being around the other dancers. I wanted to just stay at home and away from it all.

I craved sweets during that pregnancy and would consume a whole madeira cake or Sara Lee chocolate cake on a regular basis. Lynette flew down and stayed with me to await the birth. All through that pregnancy I had recurring dreams that I would leave my baby in various places and by the time I remembered and went looking for it, he or she would be dead. One night I had such a bad dream that I woke up in a sweat. I looked over to where Sheridan was sleeping on a mattress on the floor. She appeared to be sitting on her knees as if kneeling, as if she was in prayer. And she shone. There was this white light radiating from her. I sat there just looking at her for a while before going back to sleep.

Justice Athailpun was born in February 1995. She was over eight pounds and extremely difficult to push into the world. Once more that huge watermelon feeling overwhelmed me. But Justice came in less time than Sheridan. I'll never forget that first moment she was out and handed to me. It was almost as if she did not want to be here. Nevertheless, she had joined our little family and Sheridan had a little sister.

'Which way, we go back home?' Dan asked.

'Yeah, I think so, I reckon it's time. We've got two now, it'll be much easier to grow them up back home.'

Once more the decision was made to head back home to Napranum. We packed up all we had accumulated over the past couple of years in Cairns and headed off to the airport. Our luggage stretched from the check-in counter almost to the door. I'm still not sure why we weren't charged for all that excess baggage. Maybe the attendant was so shocked he couldn't think straight.

Nursing a baby the second time around was much easier. Sheridan was off to kindergarten and becoming much more independent and far less clingy with me. Regardless of her sooky face, Justice was such a contented baby, nowhere near as demanding as Sheridan had been. She very rarely cried. As long as she had her little thumb and a cushion or pillow to rub the corners of she was fine.

I slowly got back into performing – choreographing and directing the Jessica Point State School entries for the Croc Eisteddfod. These opportunities allowed me to reconnect with the community and contribute my talent and expertise, as well as helping the students to engage creatively and productively. The work also provided me with some spare cash and assisted in getting my body back into shape. I was also spending much time with Nan, documenting through print and voice recordings the knowledge and information she continued to impart at her own pace. I was always on standby. I began to dabble in painting too. I started painting anything and everything I could get my hands on: the doors and walls of the house, our furniture and also pottery. I made contact with a local non-Indigenous potter and we struck up a deal. She whipped up and sold in bulk to me pots, vases and plates of various designs and shapes, some designed by me and some that were standard. I painted them and sold the majority of these at local festivals, fetes and shops, and gave away the specially designed ones to families and friends.

I became increasingly aware of the local traditional politics in the community, as well. In particular the impact they were having not only on Nan but us as a family group. I noticed how Nan was often left out of certain 'land business' meetings and wondered why this was so. I knew Nan wasn't part of the more popular 'local granny gang' but I thought at least she had a right to be present at these meetings, especially if issues regarding her nation and country were being addressed. Surely these people would have the decency to do the right thing, I thought. I smelled a rat in the goings on of decision-making and as a result I inevitably became caught up in it all. Meetings, fights, challenges, questions and confrontations became regular occurrences. My political streak, which I had obviously inherited, really began to rear its head. Whether it was local elders, land-council representatives, lawyers, anthropologists, historians or Rio Tinto representatives my mouth was as active as ever. The process really began to consume me. I made it my business – well, actually, it was my business – to speak actively on behalf of my nan. My nan was being treated unfairly and disrespectfully. I sort of felt it was time to put to use the teachings she had been gradually handing over to me. Somehow the season to implement this knowledge had arrived. I became very vocal, was often on the local news and was always prepared for backlash.

The doubt about whether Danny really loved me kept surfacing. In fact, I wondered if we really loved each other. We had gotten married so early into our relationship. Did we really know each other at all? There were things about Danny that I was uncomfortable with and they began to really get under my skin. In one way we were happy, blissfully so, but some nagging feeling lingered inside of me.

One day I decided to address it.

'Danny?' I began.

'Yeah?'

'Danny, do you love me?'

'Yep.'

'How do you know?'

'I just do.'

'Yeah, what makes you so sure?'

He looked at me. 'Fiona, where is this coming from?'

'I just want to know. I feel like you just married me out of convenience. You always said you wanted to marry either an Asian or an Aboriginal woman who knew her culture. Well, I think that maybe you married me just because I fit that criteria.'

Silence.

'Danny?'

'Yes Fiona.' He let out a big breath.

'Would you fight for me if something challenging presented itself?'

He remained quiet.

'Well, would you?'

'Fiona, I shouldn't have to.'

'Why not?'

'I just don't think I have to, that's all.'

My doubts persisted.

The other business that was nagging me was the need to connect with my biological father. It felt stronger than ever before. Once more I began to ask questions of both Nan and Mum. Surely they had more answers for me than they were actually letting on. Maybe they'd been waiting for me to get older before they told me. Maybe they thought I wouldn't be able to handle the truth. Maybe they just needed to be prompted. What sort of man was my father? I wondered. Was he mean or kind? What did he look like, and did I look like him? My curly blonde hair must come from him. It was time to really search.

This time around Mum and Nan didn't appear to discourage me. In fact, their response was much calmer. It was always a 'Well if you want to, bubba', or 'It's not going to be easy, he could be anywhere, you know'. Mum began telling me stories about my father that made her smile. She'd laugh as she recalled these memories and shared them with me. One day I caught her in a particularly relaxed yarning mood.

'Mum, yarn to me a bit about you and my father.'

After a moment's pause she began. 'When I worked for Mr and Mrs Scanlan at Rocky Point there I would often see your father driving past. I'd just sit out the back and hope to catch a glimpse of him driving by in his car. I would hope he'd look over my way and when he did I knew then that he knew I was watching him.'

I waited for more but she didn't continue. I smiled at Mum, grateful that she had decided to share this with me. At least I didn't feel as if I'd just dropped out of the sky anymore. There was some sense to my existence; I wasn't a complete mistake. I felt validated in a way by Mum's joy as she allowed me to see the shy girl she must've been during that brief but clearly exciting courtship. But there was one story that stood out in particular, the one about where I was conceived.

CHAPTER TWELVE

Danny was sitting at the foot of the bed as I slowly woke.

'Today's the day,' I said.

'Ay? What you talking about?'

'Today's the day!' I repeated.

'Yeah Fiona, for what?'

He'd say my full name if he was impatient, cut or annoyed with me. Otherwise it'd always be 'babe'.

'Today I'm gonna start looking for that man that's biologically responsible for me.'

He paused for a moment. 'Yeah go on,' he prompted.

'Well, that's it. I'm gonna start looking today. I reckon that before that sun goes down I'm gonna find him, you watch.'

My first point of contact was Mr Egan, an Irishman who had previously lived on the community and worked as the Department of Community Services manager when I was growing up in the seventies. He was probably my best bet. I picked up the phone and dialled Comalco's administration building in the hope that the switchboard would connect us. It wasn't long before he answered in his deep Irish accent.

'Hello Mr Egan, this is Fiona here, Jean's granddaughter.'

'Oh hello there, girl. What you be ringing me for? Your grandmother put you up to this hey?'

I couldn't stand it when whitefellas used 'be' in the wrong context. Be, when used in this way, is similar to bin and is a substitute term for past tense. It's incorrect when used in present or future tense. I ignored this and attempted to explain the reason for my phone call.

'No Mr Egan, Nan got nothing to do with this. Can you tell me anything about my father?'

Slight pause.

'I see, I've been waiting for this question since you were a wee little one, you know. Put the kettle on and have hot damper waiting for me, I'll be down in ten minutes.'

I didn't knead so I sent word for Mum to send some damper down, explaining the reason why. My heart was thumping as I heard his car pull up out the front.

'Hello hello young lady,' he sang when he climbed our stairs, puffing on his beloved pipe. How are we today?' He reached into his shirt pocket. 'This is what I have for you.' He handed me a piece of paper.

Fred Wirrer Plant Op.

D.O.B 3/5/39

Dates with CAL 3/6/66 – 20/8/71

Born in Austria

To Don Egan.

'So, what brings you to this point, Fiona?'

'What do you mean, Mr Egan?'

'Why have you decided to look for Fred now?'

I shrugged. 'It's time I suppose.'

We continued on with small talk before he needed to get back to the office.

'I suggest you pay Dinny Smith a visit when you can. He is expecting you. I've already made mention of this, ay?'

'Thank you, Mr Egan.'

'Oh, and good luck with it all,' he called back with a wave.

I watched him drive off. My timing was right.

At Mr Egan's suggestion I paid Dinny Smith a visit. I entered his office with butterflies in my stomach and quietly sat in the chair opposite him. I could not believe the man in front of me knew my father.

'What I remember about your father is he had huge hands. He was a quiet, big fella and his hands were quite noticeable.'

I just sat there in shock, quite numb.

'Your father kept to himself but he did have a best friend. I think he may be able to help you.'

He waited for a response from me, but I just continued to just stare at him.

'I've spoken to him, Fiona.'

My eyes widened. Can he tell me where my father is? 'Is my father still alive?'

He smiled and nodded.

'John Foss suggests you write a letter to your father explaining everything. Send it to him and then at an opportune time he will forward it on.'

'Why do I have to send the letter to him? That will just delay everything. Why can't I just deal with Fred Wirrer directly?'

'There is the possibility that your father's married to someone who may not necessarily welcome you. This is for your own sake. I agree with Mr Foss. Take his advice and approach this carefully.'

Reluctantly I nodded in agreement.

'Great! Mr Foss lives in Western Australia with his family. He'll call you later today to sort out the process from here on.' I shook his hand.

'Oh Fiona.'

I turned around.

'The company will be able to provide you with some counselling assistance if you feel you need to talk to someone about this journey you are embarking on. If and when you decide to use it is totally up to you. The offer is there.'

'Thank you, I appreciate it,' I responded before making my exit.

The rest of the day was a blur as I just silently waited for that phone call. When he rang, John explained to me that my father was still alive and lived in Gosford, NSW, with his wife. John had regular contact with Fred and would ensure contact between us was established. John gave me his own address and phone number, so that we could stay in touch.

I hung up the phone in a state of total shock. The sun was just sinking – magnificent sunset. Before *ngar* disappeared behind the horizon, I had discovered not only that my father was alive but where he lived. I had achieved what I set out to do that morning. Tracking the footprints of my father had successfully come to pass.

'Not bad, Fiona Doyle, not bad at all woman,' exclaimed Danny as we got ready for bed that night.

'It was time, wasn't it?' I whispered.

'I reckon it must've been, go to sleep now, you've had a pretty full-on day.'

I had just made spaghetti bolognaise and was serving some up for Justice who was about two years old at the time and sitting patiently in her high chair. That girl really loved her food. Nan was also with me that day when the phone rang.

'Can you get that, Nan?' She slowly made her way over to the wall phone and after several seconds of just holding it in her hands decided to answer it.

'*Iyong in wer eh*?' she answered.

For some reason Nan would think every single person on the other end would be Wik speaking.

Without responding to the caller she turned to me and continued on, but this time in Alngith.

'*Ah, njumam nitha lin*,' as she motioned for me to grab the phone.

'Hello, this is Fiona.'

'Fiona, this is your father . . . Fred Wirrer.'

My head spun, my belly jumped. Time stood still.

The moment had arrived. It was mine to live and embrace and breathe. By the end of the call it had been decided that Fred would make a trip to Weipa as soon as possible and his wife would accompany him.

I hung up the phone in a daze, digesting the fact that I had just heard the voice of my father for the first time ever.

'About time,' was all Nan could say.

It had been two weeks since I had first spoken to Fred Wirrer on the phone. Here I was with Justice plonked on my hip watching the Fokker Friendship aircraft circle for landing. My flesh and blood on my Austrian side, the person who had only ever been a name to me all my life was on that plane. In minutes I would see him.

So many things had happened since my decision that morning to look for him. I'd had conversations with his friend, John, who had initially established contact between us. I had also exchanged several more letters with John, as well as some with Fred. Consequently, I had some idea of the sort of person he was and what to expect. Apparently his wife was no easy person to get along with at the best of times and, I was warned, was quite cantankerous by nature. I'd also realised early on that Fred's friend was not only trying to figure out where I fitted in the picture – as he did not know about Fred's affair with my mother – but also wanted to protect me from any unpleasantries that may arise.

Some of the letters that my father had written informed me of how he came to be living in Australia. After running into some trouble with bank payments on his farm back in Austria, he had decided to leave his home country and get work on a ship selling sheep to Middle Eastern countries. After overindulging on a life at sea he decided to jump ship at Port Adelaide in 1964. He opened a café, calling it Fred's Café, somewhere in Western Australia. He soon tired of that, sold up, jumped on a train and worked his way up north looking for work. He ended up in Weipa where he remained until the early seventies.

I would have preferred it that his wife didn't come with him on this initial trip, but dared not suggest it. So I was secretly glad when it turned out she didn't. I just wanted to spend time with my father on our own at this initial contact. My worst fear had been that Fred would've responded with an 'I don't know an Annie George'. But, much to my joy, the man whose name up until then was all I had as kin, was turning out to be more than what I'd hoped for. I'd set out just to find him, let him know I was alive, and hopefully hear him say that he remembered my mother and accepted that I was biologically his. That would've been enough. Yet, here I was, about to meet him in person – so much more than I had ever expected or imagined. In subtle ways, Nan and Mum had always tried to discourage me from seeking him out. Even Mr Egan warned that I should prepare myself for rejection, saying that my father may not want to have an association with me of any type. Oddly enough, none of my family members said anything about my pursuing Fred Wirrer or even commented on his visit. Dan offered no opinion. I'm sure everyone felt that this was about me and me alone. It had taken me all this time to get to this point, to confront and address the situation, and for a little black girl from a small community to successfully track down her white father was a big accomplishment in itself. Still, I think everybody was just holding their breath for what lay ahead.

I knew the tall, white-haired man the minute he appeared. He appeared in the door wearing a hat and a long-sleeved blue cotton shirt. He stood there for a couple of seconds at the top of the steps. I could tell he was embracing the moment. He had last placed his feet on this soil, what, almost twenty-five years ago. He scanned the area and focused in my direction. A couple of seconds ticked past before he slowly reached for his hat and positioned it over his heart. Someone from behind must've nudged him and, jolted back to reality, he proceeded to slowly descend the stairs, still keeping his focus on Justice and me. We just kept looking at each other as he made his way toward us. I knew who he was. He didn't have to introduce himself to me. I could see it in his face; his eyes told me that this was my blood. I had found my father and he had journeyed back to the place where it had all started for me.

Nan and *Thy* Irene Jankai, a faithful relative of ours and constant companion to Nan, were sitting in the backyard as we pulled up to 1 Peppan Street. There was no need for introductions. These two women knew exactly who this man was. Nothing much was said among the three of them, but it was not an uncomfortable silence, more like a settling into the moment.

I placed a chair behind Fred and beckoned him to sit. He joined the two elders quietly. I had no idea what Fred was feeling or thinking about the place. I didn't really care. I wanted him to see how I lived, who and what my people were. They were the ones who had given me a name, loved me, cared for me, fed me and offered some sort of identity for me to embrace.

I had freaked out earlier when I first realised he was coming, and allowed myself to become concerned about what he might think of me. The ugly spirit of unjustified shame had taken over.

As a result, I painted the room on the veranda and attempted to make it as comfortable as possible in case Fred may want to stay with us. I then painted the front door and when that failed to impress I literally chopped it off its hinges, picked it up and flung it over the veranda. But I quickly came to the conclusion that my father should accept me for who and what I was. If he didn't, it was his loss. I had people around me who loved me just the way I was. If I wasn't going to be acceptable to him then I would continue to hold my head up high, embrace this life and live it to the best of my ability with or without him, as I had done to date anyway. So I ceased trying to impress and decided to let things happen naturally, whatever the outcome would be.

Mum must've received news through the local grapevine that Fred had arrived and she turned up a little later. Fred acknowledged Mum's arrival by standing to his feet as she entered through the gate. He cupped her hand between his.

'Hello Annie, it's been a while,' he said ever so gently.

Mum just nodded. 'Nice to see you Fred.'

I placed a chair down for Mum to join us. Everyone else sat quietly and let the moment take place. Small talk unfolded. Did you have a good flight? How long are you here for? Nice to see you after all this time.

'Well, I need to get down to the *Rrutchuk* grounds. Fay can you drop me off?'

Fred quickly stood to his feet. 'Please allow me to, Annie.'

Mum looked at me. I nodded.

'Ok, thank you,' was her humble reply.

'I shouldn't be too long,' Fred said as he beckoned Mum to the hire car.

I embraced the moment. This was the only time I'd ever seen the two people who'd made me this close together. Later Mum repeated their conversation to me:

'Annie, I am so very sorry . . . for everything.'

Pause.

'It's alright, Fred. You are here now, better late than never.'

'Is there anything I could do for you, anything that you want from me?'

'No, not really, just give me a lift down to the festival grounds?'

'Of course, Annie, no problem.'

I waited impatiently for Fred's return. As soon as he entered the lounge he picked Justice up. She kept staring at her grandfather. When he sat down the chair broke beneath them. I helped Fred up and suggested the couch instead. Justice scrambled over to where I was sitting and jumped onto my lap. I handed him a poem I had written especially for this day.

Today is good
It's the first time we meet
Time has run its course
Fate has come to pass
Miracles do happen
Mountains have been removed
Now you're not just a name
But someone who is real
A special bond has begun to grow
Something real
Something new
Bloodline found . . . pieces mended

My long, long search
has now ended

'What do you think of grandad?' I whispered to Justice, as we waited for him to finish reading.

'He looks like a big king.'

'You haven't called me Dad yet,' Fred tipped his glasses down and peered over them at me. 'Why not?'

I shrugged. 'Am I allowed to?'

He let out a big chesty laugh, just like a king in fact. 'I am your father, why wouldn't you?'

'Ok,' was all I could manage in response.

Silence.

'Would you like to go see Sheridan . . . Dad?'

He smiled. 'I would like that.'

Five minutes later we drove into the *Rrutchuk* grounds and found a place to park. I could see the Napranum preschool children playing in the centre of the grounds.

'You have to guess which one she is,' I said.

He squinted toward where the little ones were and after awhile the biggest grin climbed across his face. 'Ooh, she's a bossy little one, ay?'

There she was dressed as an angel with a halo above her head yelling and bossing the other children around, both hands placed firmly on her hips.

'Is that her?' he asked, pointing.

'Yep, that's Sheridan alright.'

Later that evening Dad picked me up for dinner. He had suggested we take some time away from the rest of the family to talk. There were questions that needed to be asked, and the process was pretty overwhelming. We sat in the beer garden and watched the sunset through the tall ghost gums that line the swamp behind the Albatross Hotel. A gecko called out in the silence.

'That's a funny bird call, I haven't heard that one before.'

'That's because it's not a bird, Dad.'

'Are you sure? It sounds like a bird.'

'It's *oolay paanj*. Gecko.'

'Oh, really?'

'Yes, really!'

Silence.

'I will put money aside for the two girls for when the time comes for them to pay for their education.'

I shrugged. 'If you want to, Dad, yeah that would be great.'

Dad kept yarning and yarning, story after story, all evening. There was so much to tell. A lot of his yarns ran parallel to what Mum had told me over the years. One story stood out in particular. I had been sharing some of my childhood memories with him and mentioned Cool Pool as one of my favourite swimming holes. Dad's face lit up.

'I took your mother there, you know.' He had an excited, cheeky look in his eyes.

Eeww, I thought, but I wanted confirmation of my suspicions. I had always felt that Cool Pool held special significance for me.

'That was where you were made.'

Yeah, enough already, Dad, I wanted to say. But I could tell he was enjoying recalling the memory. 'I know, Dad, Mum has told me all about it.'

His eyes lit up. 'Has she now?' he whispered.

'Er, well, not details. More about where you picked her up from and how you two ended up there and that it was isolated and stuff and there was no way you two would get caught by anyone, well especially Nan or Grandad.'

He nodded slowly at the memory of it all.

'I always felt that place was kinda special, you know.'

'You did?' The twinkle remained in his eyes.

'Yeah,' I nodded. 'I knew it had something to do with me in some way.'

There you go. It was confirmed. Dad's story had lined up with Mum's. What a beautiful place to have come into being, I thought.

'Uhm, Dad, are there any others?' I had to ask the question.

'Any others what?'

'Other offspring?' I clarified.

'There could be one up on Thursday Island.'

Oh my goodness, I thought to myself. It could be anyone.

'Boy or girl, do you know?'

'It could be a boy. But don't get too excited, I really didn't pay that much attention when the mother fed me the story. I was a real mongrel back then, as you know already.'

'Which family group?'

Dad told me, but only time will tell if destiny wishes to reveal this brother of mine.

After dinner Dad wanted to drive down to Rocky Point. He parked the car just in front of the *qwambrahn* tree that stood to the left of the jetty. There was a slight breeze. Dad took a deep breath.

'You see just out there,' he pointed out across the croc-infested water toward Red Beach. 'I was out with my mates in a tinny, this was in the late sixties, we lost the anchor and after a bet I drew the short straw and had to dive into the river to retrieve it.'

My eyes widened. 'And you survived and surfaced?'

'I had to. I had to make and meet you, my girl.'

Must be true, I thought to myself. The chances of not being taken by *cambahl* were very slim indeed. Fred Wirrer should not have survived that dive, no way.

'You'll be surprised at what I've survived, my girl. I'll get in as many stories as I tell before I have to leave on Monday. Yeah?'

I nodded. Now it was my father's turn to tell me stories, instead of all my grannies.

It was Saturday and the *Rrutchuk* festival was in full swing. Danny and I would both be performing that evening. Dan was in charge of the running the Youth Centre at the time and, consequently, was heavily connected with the community. As a result, we'd been invited to present something at the festival, so we decided to work with a couple of locals from the community and present three pieces. There was a group piece comprising of Danny, me, another Naisda-trained dancer and a talented young boy and girl from the community. I performed a solo as well as a duet with the other female dancer. All these pieces were contemporary in approach and style, and fused mainly modern and hip-hop techniques.

Once Dad arrived at the festival we decided to go for a walk to the beach. I noticed community folk were particularly interested in what they were seeing. It was obvious that the local people who knew my story realised who this tall, white man was. The girls kept staring at their grandad, especially Justice. She could not take her eyes off him. It was obvious she was trying to figure out who exactly this big whitefella was. Of course, I thought, she had only known white people as others. Family was a different colour, yet here we were telling her that this white man was Grandad.

We sat on the beach overlooking the Embley River for as long as it took to just be. A white car drove past and hands stuck out the window and waved. Mum and her gang from the church were obviously having a *dorri* – having a good look at us.

Dad told me that the day John Foss rang him he had been driving along the Hume Highway listening to Christine Anu's version of the song *My Island Home*. Suddenly he realised that Christine was traditionally from the Torres Strait, which got him thinking about the baby he left behind all those years ago. He thought of how old Christine would have been by then and figured that the baby he left behind would probably be about the same age. And then his mobile rang. It was his old friend calling to tell him about my search for him. Dad reckons at that moment he almost drove off the highway.

We wrapped up our time at the beach and headed to the festival grounds to begin preparations for our performance that evening. My stepfather, who had married Mum when I was two years old, was at the gates slightly intoxicated. I had absolutely no idea how this encounter would unfold. I realised immediately he knew who Dad was. A big smile broke out on his face as he placed his bottle of poison in his left hand and extended his right hand.

'How you going there, Fred? I'm pleased to meet you. I'm Annie's husband.'

There was no way my stepfather would've done this if he was sober. Not at all. He rarely even spoke. He hadn't spoken to me all my life, never. This was obviously the grog talking. I stepped back and let them make small talk for a bit before walking off. Dad initiated a goodbye and caught up with me.

'Everything alright?'

'Yep,' I nodded.

'So he's the father of the three younger ones?'

'Yep, but he's not with Mum anymore. He's living with someone else.'

'Oh, I see.'

The rest of the evening consisted of performances, speeches, lots of eating and, of course, fireworks. Nan sat proudly alongside Dad as I performed on stage. Never would I have imagined that moment would come to pass, but my persistence had paid off. It couldn't possibly get any better than this. I had to keep pinching myself to make sure this wasn't just a dream.

The next day Dad packed a picnic lunch and he, the girls and I went to Gonbung. He told me more stories, as Sheridan and Justice played on the sand.

'Sheri, not too close to the water, crocodile might get you,' I called out to her.

She ignored me and kept playing near the shoreline.

'Sheridan, did you hear what I said? Move away from the water's edge, *cambahl* there, look.'

'No, you bastard,' she snapped back at me.

'What the – ?' was all I could say.

Dad let out this big, shocked laugh. 'She's fiery!'

'No kidding. Try living with her.'

We walked down to the point and Dad pointed out toward Pelican Island.

'I took your mother out there as well, you know.'

'Yeah yeah, Dad,' I said jokingly. 'I get the picture. It seems to be about the bush, the land and you and my mother.'

He just smiled.

'Tell us some more stories,' I said.

He adjusted his position and got comfortable.

'Well there was this one time when I had decided to leave Weipa.'

'Was this after I was made?'

'Nope. You were not even heard of. Anyway, I packed all my belongings, including the dingos, and started my journey out of Weipa. Once it started to get dark I decided to set up camp for the night so I pulled up near Myall Creek.'

I smiled.

'I assumc you know where that is?'

'Duh, Dad.'

'Of course, of course.' He smiled, nodding.

'Anyway I came across a boar pig and after shooting it I decided to string it up by the bank where I decided to sleep. I had my fire and the dingos with me for company and before I knew it I was out to it. Had a good night sleep that night, no disturbance at all.'

'So, what did you do with the boar pig after that?'

'Well nothing. You see there was no boar pig in the morning.'

'Hey?'

'Instead there were huge crocodile tracks that stopped just beneath where the pig had been hanging from the tree. The tracks doubled up, indicating it had passed me on its way back into the creek.'

My eyes widened.

'I might have taken the pig's life, but it ended up saving mine.'

'That's the second time you've cheated death when it comes to crocs, Dad. What did you do after that?'

'I decided to come back to Weipa.'

'Why?'

'You had to be made, I suppose.'

All too soon Monday arrived. This time Dad was departing the proper way. He had respectfully acknowledged the affair he had with the woman he kept stealing off with into the bush, the land of her forefathers, and he had acknowledged and accepted the seeds that resulted from that business – me and his granddaughters. Out of respect, Mum and Nan also came out to the airport to farewell Dad. I was so happy that they suggested it; I had been wrapped up in Dad all weekend and hadn't stopped to check how they were doing. It was obvious now that I had their support even if no words were exchanged.

'I'll be in touch soon. You, Dan and the girls must come down to visit as soon as it is conveniently possible.'

This was the second time he was leaving me and Weipa behind. Was I really going to see him again? Was he going to continue to be a part of my life or was he going to just disappear back into the comfortable, cushy life that he had created for himself?

CHAPTER THIRTEEN

Not long after Dad left, Danny got a job with Comalco in the regeneration section, which resulted in a house in town being offered to us. It was only about 10 or 15 kilometres away and I loved the idea. Even though Napranum was my home it was far too noisy and the constant family demands and interruptions were getting a bit much to keep up with. We moved into a house at Trunding in Weipa and settled in. I was employed at the Jessica Point State School as an intervention tutor at that stage, which was in Napranum, so, while we enrolled Sheridan at Weipa North State School in town, Justice continued to attend kindergarten at Napranum. The money from my position and the continued sales of my artwork allowed me to save while we lived off Danny's wage.

For the first time since the girls were born we had our own place, even if we didn't own it. I got stuck into the front yard and filled it with plants and several garden beds as well as tending a well-filled greenhouse that constantly released the aromatic scent of basil. It was 1996 and my life was full and happy. Dan and I were both employed, juggling the girls worked, I had Dad in my life, my relatives were just down the road, and I had a place that I could potter around and nest in. I also established a friendly association with a non-Indigenous woman in town with a dance background and we began teaching and choreographing collaboratively, as well. As soon as I met Marnie Young I liked her. She was friendly and very humble and respectful. We started talking about our connections to dance when she mentioned that maybe we should get together and perhaps play creatively. We connected so well that we decided to hold open classes for the community for both kids and adults. There was so much interest that we had to structure the classes according to ages. Soon we realised that all this training and creating should be for something. An end-of-year performance was conceived and once more dance made its way into my life. We incorporated every dance genre into the pieces from classical to tap to Indigenous fusion. Rehearsals were held at St Luke's church and the assembly hall was booked as our performance venue. So many locals contributed their support, from the provision of lighting to taking footage to decorating the hall for us. It was great to see all the white kids dressed in the colours red, black and yellow sitting around Nan who had also been incorporated into the performance. Families from Napranum came along to see the show. This was really good stuff in terms of black–white relations for Weipa.

I was nearly thirty years of age, contented and happy and blessed. And about to wrap up almost a decade of immense growth and incredible experiences since my marriage and graduation from Naisda. I'd also had a children's book published by Rams Skull Press, which was based in Kuranda, Queensland. The day I received the package with a handful of *Sandbeach Girl* I had a strong sense that I could continue telling stories through print. I knew I had a long way to go with the English language and in my ability to articulate effectively, but the fact that Ron Edwards took an interest in my writing was just what I needed to confirm and honour my commitment to the writing and publishing process. Neither *Sandbeach Girl* nor *Looking for Yams*, which was published three years later, were at the level that I would've preferred, but these books are still very special to me. They confirmed the words of Oodgeroo Noonuccal (Kath Walker) the well-known Aboriginal poet and activist whose traditional roots sit within Minjerribah, or Stradbroke Island as it is more commonly known. Oodgeroo had written to me in the early nineties encouraging me to keep writing no matter how long the journey or what obstacles life threw my way. I thought, if this woman can take the time to say this to me then surely the wind is telling me that indeed there is a place for me in the area of yarning in book form.

Dad kept insisting that we visit his family in Gosford as soon as it was conveniently possible. His wife and stepchildren apparently wanted to meet us. We weren't able to make a trip as a whole family due to work commitments, so it was decided that I would first make the trip alone. Dad bought the ticket and off I set. He and his wife Gretal were at the airport in Sydney on my arrival. My initial sense of his wife was that she was a stern, no-nonsense type. Dad had informed me that, although she may come across a little harsh, in fact she had a lot of love to offer and at the end of the day she meant well. I took note. Everything about my father was familiar to me, his presence, his spirit, his eyes and, in particular, his voice. Even his property felt like home; I don't know how else to describe this feeling of knowing or familiarity, but that is exactly how I felt.

Attempts at conversations through constant questions and answers unfolded awkwardly between Gretal, Dad's stepdaughter Beatress, Beatress's husband and me. I submitted to the unfamiliar flow of conversation between these people, but I knew from the outset that I had absolutely nothing in common with them apart from an association with Fred Wirrer. What set me apart was that my association was biological. I was, in fact, of his blood. Still, they had taken the time to come and meet me. They appeared friendly and, dare I say, 'normal' enough. I marvelled at Beatress's house at lunch the following day as she walked me from room to room.

'Wow, this place is gorgeous. Absolutely gorgeous, especially the high ceilings. Did you design this yourself?' I asked.

'My husband is a designer-builder so yes this is our own design,' she responded proudly.

The walls of one room were lined with a variety of sharp objects ranging from large knives to machetes and axes. I wondered about the fascination with such dangerous objects, but held my tongue. It gave me the creeps, but I did not know these people well enough and didn't trust myself to construct the questions I wanted to ask or phrase any comments I may have wanted to voice.

Later, as Dad and I made our way back to his place I asked how they managed to get a place like that built.

'He's sitting pretty comfortable, making good money,' was Dad's response.

He quoted an approximate amount to me. From the life I've always known, I couldn't even begin to imagine an income stream at that level.

'Tell me about Christine Anu. Do you know her, Princess?' Dad enquired one day as we sat in the lounge room relaxing.

'Of course I know her, why?' The question both surprised and annoyed me for some reason.

'I think she's fantastic.'

'Yeah, well, she's certainly talented, Dad, and very clever too.'

I could tell he wanted to talk more.

'Have you seen her shots in the latest magazine? I'm not sure what it's called now.' I knew which ones he was referring to. Christine had recently done some nude photos, which, personally, I thought were excellent but just knowing that my dad had seen them as well kind of made me uncomfortable.

'Aagh Dad, what the . . . ?'

He laughed. 'Fiona your old man does know what art is. Those photos aren't wrong in any way. In fact, they're very tastefully done,' he said with a cheeky grin.

I still felt weird though.

'Yeah, yeah, you could say that, Dad.' I smiled, realising that sitting in front of me was a huge Christine Anu fan.

I really understood what I had let myself in for when Dad proudly presented photos of Sheridan and Justice to his mother-in-law. She took hold of the one of Justice and, after studying it intently, proceeded to hand it back to Dad.

'I've always wanted to get meself one of *those*,' she said, with an accent that made my skin crawl and belly turn.

Dad grabbed the photo from her and suggested he and I take a walk through the property.

Most of the next two days was spent on walks outdoors. Dad, myself and Tess the dog used the time to continue to bond. Dad's wife never attempted to join us. I didn't mind though, it provided more time for us to yarn without any interruptions. The property had been well planned. Roses, over a hundred and forty odd, greeted you on entry. Citrus trees sat like soldiers beside them surrounded by a variety of flowers and shrubbery of different sorts and colours.

To the back of the property numerous gardens consisting of, but not limited to, palms, ferns, begonias, Australian natives and so on led you further down to the creek that backed onto a small waterfall that tumbled down into it. On the rise to the left of the main garden area was a smorgasbord of vegetable gardens and further up on the slope pear trees laden with fruit greeted us.

'Come in here, my girl,' Dad beckoned me into one of the vegetable patches. 'Would you like some strawberries? Help me look.'

Dad found some, gave them a bit of a clean and dropped them into my hand. I remembered the strawberry birthmark on my neck and took special note of the moment. It was an anointed time, I believed, predestined for me to inhale and embrace. On our way back I noticed a clay statue of a girl in the garden among the ferns and orchids.

'Hey, there's Nyrlotte,' I teased, pointing to the statue.

'We shall know her as Nyrlotte from this day on,' Dad replied appearing impressed with my association. 'So what do you think, my girl?'

'About what?'

'About what I've done here.'

I didn't answer. I couldn't. I was overwhelmed by what he had created, of all my father had achieved after jumping ship illegally all those years back with no money and not a word of English in his vocabulary. Not bad at all.

'It's beautiful, Dad. Don't know what to say except that, well, it's pretty cool what you've done really.'

Dad smiled.

'I'll name her after you.'

'Hey?'

'This place, this area. I'll call her Fiona's Country. Would you like that?'

That took me by surprise. I just smiled.

'This could all be yours, you know.'

'It'll be a lot of work, Dad,' I joked.

'You're not wrong, girl. It'll keep Danny busy, that's for sure.'

Slowly but surely the attitude of Dad's wife became more and more stand-offish toward me. She rarely engaged in conversation and when she did her voice had an aggressive, somewhat irritated tone. Whenever I felt uncomfortable at something she said or did I reminded myself of what Dad told me – that she meant well and that regardless of how she may come across she possessed a good heart. Besides, I didn't want to waste time and energy on the little bit of negativity that kept rearing its head whether real or perceived; there was much more important business, like getting to know Dad and spending time with him, that deserved my focus, energy and attention.

One evening we were sitting in the dining room engaged in conversation when Dad disappeared into his room and returned with a plastic bag in his hand.

'You remember you asked for something of your grandmother's, Princess?'

'Yep,' I replied, slightly curious.

When I had first made contact with Dad on the phone I had asked him if he had anything of his mum's that could be passed onto me. I had always suspected a familiar spirit had been constantly close to me throughout my life, particularly during my childhood. It was becoming increasingly evident that this familiar spirit was most probably my Austrian granny, Anna Wallman – one of the women on my European lineage.

'Well, I have something for you. I rang my brother in Austria and after going through the family trunk this is what he dug out.'

He handed me a well-preserved piece of cloth.

'What is it?'

'Your grandmother stitched this when she was just sixteen years old, in 1925.' I made a mental note that my Aboriginal nan was also born in 1925, while Dad proceeded to explain the various symbols that made up the red design. In the middle of the cloth, surrounded by four stars and a flower design, the family crest was stitched along with more flower designs on each corner.

'Wow Dad, I don't know what to say.'

He looked at me and smiled.

'It's yours now. Your grandmother would've wanted you to have it.'

He unfolded the cloth and spread it out on the table. My granny had stitched the following onto it:

Maria ilt de Stern, Der unfer Leben lengt,

Bu der Geimath fern, Die uns der Gimmellfenkt

19AW25

(the year she stitched the cloth and her initials AW, Anna Wallmann)

One day, Dad and I were in the car on our way somewhere when I decided to ask him something that was niggling at me. I knew I had to get the question out while I had the chance, especially since he had presented me with the cloth.

'Dad, would your mum have accepted me?' Dad kept his eyes on the road ahead.

'Of course she would've. She would've loved you. She would've recognised you. You have her nose and my father's mouth. Even Gretal noticed that you look like your grandmother, especially in the nose and cheek area.'

I felt relieved. A mixed bag of emotions ran through me, but the strongest was relief, it felt soft and soothing deep inside my belly place.

All too soon the visit came to an end. Gretal decided to come to the airport. I waved goodbye and made my way to the departure lounge. We had decided that it wasn't necessary for them to wait with me until I boarded. They had a long drive back to Gosford.

'Make sure you, Dan and the girls come back soon, okay?'

I nodded and waved, noticing that Gretal had already turned around and had begun to make her way back to the front of the airport without saying goodbye. I had really wanted to farewell her respectfully and thank her for her hospitality, such as it was. I did not understand why she had been so uptight and cold. There'd been no smiles, laughter, or warmth from her for the entire time I was there. She was so straight and systematic, almost like a soldier. She did not appear to love or appreciate love, joy, laughter or just being in the moment. How could someone live like this? How dry would your heart and spirit be? I imagined her heart must've looked like a dried-up old prune. Maybe she just doesn't like goodbyes, I told myself, preferring to believe in something promising, for Dad's sake at least.

I returned back to Weipa with my identity a lot fatter. Dad had given me photos of his family going back generations. There were also historical records and genealogies. By this stage I knew we also had Jewish and Viking ancestry. My grandfather, Dad's father, had gone missing during the war in the forties somewhere in the snow on the border of Russia and Germany. His body was never found. My grandmother, Anna, had remained unmarried until the day she passed.

Dad had told me how my Austrian granny secretly helped wounded soldiers, who stumbled into the farm looking for a place to hide and recover. She would allow them to remain in the stable at the back and would feed them bread and water and tend to their wounds until they were ready to move on. Dad emphasised my granny's bravery, attributing it to her incredibly strong Catholic faith, and noted the similarity between her strength and stubbornness and that of my maternal grandmother.

It wasn't long before my whole family was able to travel down to Gosford. Fortunately, Dan's work with Rio Tinto (formerly Comalco) provided us with a travel fund that made life just that little bit easier. It covered airfares and land travel as well as accommodation costs, although Dad had offered his place if we wanted to stay there. So all we needed to budget for was spending money and food.

One day before we set off, I rang Dad, rather than wait for his daily call. To my surprise Gretal answered the phone.

'Fred's not here. What do you want?' she asked. 'You know he's known about you all along?' Her voice dropped.

'He did mention it.'

She butted in quickly. 'Yeah, well, the more he ignored you the easier it got for him.'

I was feeling quite confused and uncomfortable by now. I didn't know where she was coming from, but I sensed a spirit of subtle attack underneath her words.

'And did you know your father was an atrocious alcoholic?' she continued.

'Uhm, actually no, he hasn't said anything on those lines . . . although –'

'Well, he was, real terrible he was,' she interrupted once more. 'I put up with so much of his nonsense, it was shocking, absolutely shocking. At night he would . . .' And she went on to reveal information that I was surprised she would want to share.

By the time I hung the phone up I felt sick. I'd been caught totally off guard. It took a while for her words to sink in.

When I told Danny about the call his immediate response was, 'We're not staying with her. Ring your father and explain why.'

There was silence as I told Dad what happened. I repeated what she had said to me. By this stage she had joined in the conversation and I had been put on speaker phone.

'Well it's true, Fred, even you said that Annie was just to pass the time away.'

'How could you be so cruel?' Dad snapped.

I could not speak.

'Dad, I have to go,' I managed to say, fighting hard to hold the tears back. 'We'll visit but we won't be staying with you.'

A week later we checked into a hotel by the water in Gosford. It wasn't flash, but at least we had our own space. On our arrival at Dad's place the reception was cold. For the entire time we were there no other family member came to say hello. Gretal rarely spoke and seemed completely uninterested in us. The girls, of course, were completely oblivious to this. They were having too much fun with their grandad as he drove them around the property on his ride-on mower and fed them fresh oranges from his orchard. For the duration of our visit Gretal did not accompany us on any outings. I really didn't care, though. Dad displayed so much love and attention to us. It warmed me incredibly to see the girls interact and communicate with their grandad. This was why I had needed to look for him and have him in my life. We were, at last, a part of each other's lives; not even the negatives of his family members could rob us of that joy.

By the end of that trip, though, I knew exactly where I stood with my father's wife. What I couldn't understand was what business was it of his other family members? How could they justify their resistance of my entering the picture?

The day before we left we went shopping. Dad carried Justice on his shoulder. Sheridan had gone off with Danny and was running excitedly from section to section of the huge store – how shop deprived we were as a result of living in Weipa.

'Princess?'

I looked at Dad.

'I have changed my will to include you and the girls.' He took a deep breath and exhaled. 'So when the time comes you and the girls will get something.'

I kept walking, looking at the various items on display.

'I want you to know that Beatress's boys are still included. They've grown up knowing me as Pop.'

I nodded.

'Well how do you feel about that?'

'It's your choice, they've grown up with you.'

'Okay, that's settled then.'

Dad rang every single day to see how we were going.

'I love you so much that it hurts,' he would say.

But it wasn't always positive, loving conversations. We had

some pretty challenging arguments. As well as voicing his objection to religion, Dad did not approve of Danny's hunting of wild game.

'I just don't see why he'd want to shoot those poor innocent animals, there really isn't any need to anymore.'

'Dad, it's cultural. Danny loves going bush and hunting for bush tucker. He hunts for food for Nan as well.'

'And Nan allows it?'

'Of course, she actually prefers to eat bush tucker. She hates meat from the butcher.'

Rather than progress into heated dialogue we would conclude with a 'let's agree to disagree'. But I didn't understand how he appeared incapable of understanding things from a cultural perspective – him, of all people. I didn't even see Dad as a white man. When he arrived in this country, all he had was a little, red German-to-English dictionary. He had slowly built his vocab up, and was now a man of language and culture. Surely he would understand, but he didn't appear to. It upset me. I wanted him to understand and agree with me, but he didn't. We also locked horns constantly about my Christian faith. Dad made it clear he was a man of science and logic and stated that religion was the reason war existed. I could not relate to his atheism at all. We avoided discussing my faith and his beliefs as much as possible – unless we were up for a verbal slinging match, of course.

'Guess what, Princess?' Dad piped into the phone one day. 'I switched to Labor.'

'Oh okay, why?'

'Well, no use voting Liberal anymore is there? My descendants are Aboriginal. What does Liberal do for your people?'

I wanted to ask him why he had been voting Liberal in the first place but didn't feel up to a debate.

'Well that's great, Dad,' was all I could manage. 'Really good.'

'Yep and Gretal has joined as well.'

'That's even better, Dad. Great in fact.'

'Yeah, yeah, I thought so too.'

CHAPTER FOURTEEN

'Guess what?' I said excitedly to Danny as he drove into the driveway late one afternoon after work.

'What up woman?'

'Naisda's having a reunion. I got an email from Monica Stevens. I think we should go down.'

It had been about eight years or so since we had seen anyone from our Naisda days and I was curious about the other dancers and wanted to reconnect somehow. Dan grabbed his work bag and started dusting his work boots on the driveway cement.

'What you reckon?'

Dan appeared absent-minded. 'Hey, 'bout what?'

''Bout what I just told you. Do you wanna go?'

'Can't afford it, besides whose gonna look after the kids ay?'

That stopped me in my tracks for a bit. Later that evening I picked up the subject again.

'Don't you wanna meet up with that mob again? Aren't you just a tad bit curious of where and how everyone's turned out?'

'Yeah, but I don't think I can get the time off work and then there's the money thing. Maybe you can just go.'

It turned out that Naisda was able to pay for me and we were able to purchase a ticket for Sheridan to come as well. Dad drove down to Sydney and spent the couple of days with us. I couldn't wait to reconnect with everyone. I was so excited.

Entering the venue I noticed none other than Christine Anu herself talking to someone in the lobby. The biggest smile spread across Dad's face.

'Please introduce your old father to her.'

'Stop it, you're going to embarrass me.'

I made my way over to her. There was no harm in introducing Dad to her.

'Which way?' I hugged her. 'Christine, Dad – Dad, Christine.'

'Hello, Fiona's dad,' she grinned and extended her hand toward him.

Dad shook her hand enthusiastically and we exchanged small talk before I proceeded upstairs.

The reunion was not as I had expected. The energy and spirit just didn't seem the same as in the days when I had trained. There were also a lot of new faces around. Even the teachers from the mid to late nineties appeared to be distant in their attitude. I expected a lot of singing, dancing, laughter and reminiscing of the old days, but there wasn't any. And I felt let down that most of the members of my group hadn't attended. Still, it was nice to connect with the few that did and it was midnight by the time I left.

'Wow, I can't believe I actually met her,' Dad said as we drove back to the hotel.

By now I was becoming a regular at Dad's place, although Dad had mentioned that the only reason Gretal's family turned up that first time was out of curiosity. They were not interested in accepting me as family. This did not really bother me, but I did wonder what it must be like for Dad dealing with this mob every day.

'Tony doesn't talk to me at all,' he confided. 'Sally still does, but even she has somewhat changed. The youngest boy still visits, the older two don't anymore.'

I could hear the pain in his voice.

'I'm really sorry this has happened to you.'

'This is not your fault, Princess. I am so glad you and the girls are in my life. It is now complete.'

'But why they are like this? It doesn't make any sense.'

'Maybe greed. They are obviously threatened by you and the girls.'

'But they already have everything they would ever want let alone need. What I've got doesn't come close. Why would they feel threatened to this extent?'

'Like I said, my girl, greed, greed and control.'

I was flabbergasted. The behaviour of these people absolutely spun me out. This woman and her family had had my father in their lives for over twenty years. Now it was our turn, for me and the girls to experience this blessing. To have Dad's voice and presence as part of our lives.

Life continued on following that business. Dad and I

continued to speak every day on the phone. I really don't like talking on the phone, but, of course, I looked forward to his calls. It was like he was trying to make up for lost time, for twenty-seven years to be exact.

I was still working as an intervention tutor at the Jessica Point State School when I bit into a mandarin one lunch time and a seed cracked my tooth. Well, the drama that erupted from that! Before I knew it Dan, the girls and I were on the next available flight out to Cairns to get my tooth fixed as soon as possible. There was no way I was going to remain in Weipa and carry on as per usual with a cracked tooth. Shame job!

We flew out on a Friday afternoon and had to wait until Monday for me to be seen. We hired a car and decided to take a drive up to Port Douglas on the Saturday. Before long I began to feel extremely nauseous.

'You're pregnant, woman.'

'Of course I'm not, Danny, you silly. It's this bloomin' windy road that's freaking my head and stomach out.'

I was twenty-nine years old and had always said that I wouldn't be having any more babies once I turned thirty. I wasn't on any contraception, but had managed to get away with it for the past three years or so. No way did I want a baby now; Sheridan and Justice were enough.

At Port Douglas Danny rushed into a chemist, exiting with a home pregnancy kit.

'Here, just take the test when we get back to the hotel just to make sure.' He threw the packet onto my lap.

I just sat there in our hotel room staring at the blue cross on the stick. Oh my God. Danny was right! I exited the toilet and handed the stick to him.

'How did you know?'

'I planned it in the kitchen that night,' he boasted with the biggest, cheekiest grin on his face.

I remembered that session in the kitchen that night, too.

'Not funny, Danny, no joke. I'm turning thirty next year, what the hell?'

'So, you're having the baby before it's too late then aren't ya?'

'Easy for you to say, you don't have to carry 'em.'

Dan kept smiling as he broke the news to Sheridan and Justice. I secretly felt a twinge of excitement run through me, but opted not to reveal it just yet. All I could think of was going through the whole thing again. Justice had just started kindy and I gotten used to undisturbed sleep again. Even though during and around both pregnancies I'd kept choreographing and performing for schools and community alike, I badly wanted to focus on working and keeping my body in shape. Every year there were constant demands to work with schools for eisteddfods as well as local festivals and events. And even if I did not personally get invited to assist I would create my own opportunities and present them to relevant groups for their consideration. There were times when I thought that dance would end for me, that my involvement with the art form was over. But somehow every time, year after year, there I'd be again, involved in some performance or presentation as either performer or choreographer or both. I don't think I had a choice really; it was as if dance always had its way with me. It was the natural thing for me to do, it was just like breathing.

There was absolutely nothing wrong this time around. It was definitely a textbook pregnancy. When the time approached we booked a hotel, packed the girls up and flew to Cairns two weeks before the due date to await the baby's birth. I notified Dad who was basically on standby, promising that if I let him know immediate sign of impending labour he would be there rain, hail or shine. As I later found out, he wasn't kidding.

I literally walked myself into labour. I shopped and shopped during that first week in Cairns until my legs almost collapsed under me. Contractions began shortly after midnight following one of these daily shopping trips in the second week. I went to the toilet in the early hours of the morning and noticed the show, a telltale sign that indicates the onset of labour. I knew I'd be holding that baby by the end of the following day and I woke Dan up.

'Call Dad and tell him it's not far now.'

Ebony arrived around mid-morning on 2 June 1999, still in the sac. Against the instructions of the nurse I had apparently pushed way too early, my waters had not even broken. It looked like I had just given birth to an alien, it was the freakiest sight. Dan nipped the top of the sac under strict instruction and a watchful eye from the nurse and rolled back the placenta as the nurse pulled Ebony out. Dan then cut the umbilical cord. A couple of hours later we were pulling into our hotel with Ebony wrapped in a blanket only to find Dad checking in. I could not believe he had made it to Cairns in that time.

'*Chay*, that old fella must've been flying, that was way too quick,' whispered Danny.

'Grandad, grandad,' sang the girls excitedly once they spotted him. 'Dad let us out, we wanna go see grandad.'

Apparently Dad had immediately jumped in the car, much to his wife's resentment. He made it to Cairns on the same day. After settling into his room next door to ours, Dad officially met his latest granddaughter. When I placed her on his lap, he just stared at her. All I could think about was when I held Sheridan and Justice for the first time and wondered about him. Now he was here. It was a beautiful moment indeed. Dad just kept looking at Ebony as she lay wrapped in her blanket. He looked up at me, but remained silent. In fact, the whole room was quiet. Dan busied himself in the kitchen while Sheridan and Justice just stared at their grandad in turn. There appeared to be no need for words. Why talk when the moment being lived was sweet enough.

Ebony was a gorgeous baby and gave me no trouble at all, a beautiful little addition to our family. I had decided to return to study to gain qualifications in early childhood teaching. After making some enquiries at the Remote Area Teacher Education Program (RATEP), at the beginning of 2000 I enrolled and when Ebony was nine months old I commenced studying.

Here I was at thirty years of age with three daughters, a granny to look after, a house to run and a degree to get through. Although Dan and I had moved into town we had decided to have Nan stay with us whenever she wanted to. And I'm pretty sure she was at ours more than she was back at her own place in Napranum. In the mornings I'd get Ebony to her babysitter before heading out to Naps with Justice and Nan. Sheridan would get herself to school as it was only a ten-minute walk from our place at Tarquin Court. Once we got to the community, I'd leave Nan at

Peppan Street, take Justice to preschool and then go to the campus where I remained until the afternoon, only to do it all again the next day. My life became dramatically systematic in order to meet deadlines and fulfil my family duties. And, as if all that wasn't enough, I continued with freelance writing, and continued with choreography and performances for the school. As congested as life was, though, I still had to stay connected with the arts in this way; it was almost as if it was my fuel.

I really enjoyed the challenge of studying again. RATEP allowed me flexibility and the opportunity to work at my own pace. And the support I received from everyone involved in the course as well as the staff at the Napranum campus was excellent. I really don't think I would've been able to survive if I'd had to do the degree through the mainstream approach.

The three years between 2000 and 2002 were nothing short of a rollercoaster ride. I handed Ebony over to babysitters during the day, sadly missing out on her first steps and first words. She even called her babysitter 'Mum' for a while.

Around this time my biography of Nan's life titled *Whispers of This Wik Woman* was highly commended in the David Unaipon Award for unpublished Indigenous writers. It was suggested by the judges that I work with an Indigenous mentor who'd assist me with reworking the manuscript prior to resubmitting it the following year. My writing had slowly started to get recognised since *Sandbeach Girl* and *Looking for Yams* had been published and I was invited to the first Indigenous Writers Forum to be held in Brisbane in 2002. Here I was able to meet and yarn with writers such as Uncle Herb Wharton, Uncle Albert Holt, my mentor Melissa Lucashenko and performer Maroochy Barambah. I absolutely loved it. Up until that point it really was just me trotting along dabbling in a form and a language that was still pretty much unfamiliar to me. It had been a long and isolated process. I did not know of anyone else in my community who had an interest in writing or literature. One day Melissa and I met briefly in my hotel room for a bit of a yarn about where I was at as a developing writer.

'Who do you want your audience to be?' she asked.

'I don't know,' I shrugged. 'I don't think about it like that, I just like to write.'

'Well, your target audience determines your choice of words and your language construction. Say, for instance, you just wanted Napranum people to be your audience, your readers, then you would have an idea of how to write and which words to use. Yeah?'

I kept looking at her.

'So, your audience could either be just Napranum, or Weipa or Wik people, or Cape York, or the larger majority of Australians in general. You see what I'm saying?'

'I think so.'

'Home language is good, great in fact. But make sure you have the right balance of home language, dialect and standard Australian, yeah?'

I nodded.

'But always keep your own voice, never change that!'

Names who inspired me in the early days were Jack Davies, Kevin Gilbert, Oodgeroo Noonuccal and David Unaipon himself. Surely, there would be a place for me in this arena, I would secretly dream. Whenever I saw a black person who resembled my grandfather or uncle, aunties, mothers and grannies being recognised for whatever reason in the mainstream I would get excited, although the ones that influenced me the most were those involved in the literary and performing arts. It really did seem that it just might be possible to hold a book in my hands one day, or have an idea for a play come to life on stage, or to travel to other countries and share my story and my voice abroad.

During the forum we were invited to attend an event hosted by the Terminus in Melbourne Street, South Brisbane. Writers of various genres were scheduled to talk about their most recent publications. I soon realised there was an open mic section and decided to present some of my own writing. I was told that I would only be able to if time allowed it. Fair enough, I carried some *ochre* along with me to paint up just in case.

Fortunately there was time left over. By this stage the place had become quite rowdy, and the presenters appeared to be unable to hold the audience's attention. Regardless of the rowdy atmosphere, I painted up and made my way to the stage. I instructed the sound guy that I would like some smoke for effect once spoken word began and then waited for the audience to quieten down. When they didn't, I tapped the mic to see if it was on. It was.

'Uhm, scuse me guys but I won't be able to start unless everyone is quiet.'

Instant silence.

I felt so good up there once I started. I really, really loved being in that place. It was my first time delivering a written piece of work since my days at Naisda during the eighties. I read some extracts from a piece of work titled *Four Faces, One Blood*, which was basically about the four generations of my maternal lineage.

Old black hands
So old . . . so fine
So long fingers, so soft
Just like mountains
Those veins so high
That skin, like *paanj*
Wrinkly . . . soft
That lip . . . pink with darkened black spots
Those eyes . . . misty . . . greyish
Going blind now
Hair silvery . . . so smooth . . . so strong
Them feet . . . long . . . so straight
Planted down on ground
Love that earth
So close to myself
My being is there
Where those voices drone endlessly
Why they sing?
It's life for them
This old woman
So different . . . from me
Yet my womb is her womb
Her blood poured into me
So strange . . . this life . . .
Old Nyrlotte,
Awumpan
Athailpun
Me then
Nyrlotte

The silence remained until the last word was spoken. During the clapping I could hear a couple of women up the back cheering slightly more loudly than the rest. They later came up and introduced themselves as fellow 'Austrian Aboriginals'. Anita Heiss was one of them.

'Great stuff, sis!' They handed me their cards. 'You might be hearing from one of us at some point.'

'Okay, ta,' was all I could manage.

CHAPTER FIFTEEN

Late 2002, I got a phone call inviting me to travel to Canada as Queensland's representative to join other Indigenous writers in sharing and promoting our works with Indigenous writers from Canada, America and New Zealand. I was absolutely ecstatic! I was finally stepping into the arena.

I boarded the plane at the Weipa Airport with a swag of tickets that would track me across the Pacific Ocean and on to Vancouver. I was so excited when we neared Hawaii and I saw from the runway the word *aloha* on the airport building. It reminded me of the Elvis Presley movies I used to watch as a kid. Here I was about to place my feet on Hawaiian soil. Well, not quite, but being at the airport was close enough for now. After a break, and some lying around we reboarded and tracked onto Vancouver, Canada.

I will never forget the sight as the pilot announced our descent an hour out of the city. I lifted the window shade to feast my eyes on the most precious sight ever. The moon was positioned full and heavy above a ribbon of mountains that majestically danced over the countryside and on toward our destination. Waking up the next morning in my hotel room at Granville Island had a special sort of magic about it as well. Danny rang to check that I had made it safely and we talked for a bit, clocking up a phone bill of about $300. It was worth it though; his voice made a difference and fuelled me to make the most of this trip.

I had an interview later on that day with a television crew, so thought I better get a move on and familiarise myself with my material and the program agenda. I couldn't wait to get stuck into it all and start mixing with the other contingents. These interviews had been arranged by the organisers of the trip to give representatives and opportunity to talk to various television networks, radio stations and newspapers about their work. My interview location had me backing onto a lake, creating the deadliest backdrop. The Canadian air was crisp, clear and refreshing, very much unlike the Western Cape atmosphere I was used to. Us delegates spent roughly a week together in Vancouver, doing these interviews as well as participating in forums and presenting our works both individually and collaboratively. The festival was titled Honouring Words and created a platform for Indigenous writers to showcase their works.

The first time I heard the drums and singing of the Canadian Aboriginal people my spirit leapt with joy. I had always wanted to organically experience this atmosphere and had sensed that perhaps one day this would come to pass. Here I was actually experiencing this. I felt extremely blessed indeed to be among such people. There was one low point during our time in Vancouver, however, and that involved my fellow Australian travellers. An issue had to be dealt with regarding our travel back home and it was best we do that before we ventured off to Winnipeg and Toronto, so as to avoid any last minute dramas. Three of us needed clarification of our travel date, time and airline – the South Australian rep Kim Scott, the Victorian rep Jada Milroy and me. After some discussion it was decided that I would approach one of the organisers to discuss our options. To my surprise she responded quite rudely, appearing almost pissed off with my even taking the issue to her. The more I tried to make sense out of what she was saying, the more verbally aggressive she became. Before too long I thought, stuff this woman. I don't know who she thought she was to carry on like that so I started to then challenge her role and responsibilities regarding any business related to the trip. Next thing I knew, her colleague piped in.

'Is this community way of dealing with stuff?'

I was shocked. What the hell does this even mean? Here were these two women in high-up positions travelling all over the world representing Australian Aboriginal people and they were treating me like I was beneath them or something. Their true colours had come to the fore that night – convenient blackfella or coconut came to mind as well as blackfellas who talked the talk but didn't necessarily walk the walk. Even the contingents from Canada, America and New Zealand were appalled when they realised what had happened. Regardless, I hadn't travelled thousands of miles just to have this so-called sister taint the experience. I breathed the business out and let it go, focusing on what lay ahead.

Winnipeg sat smack bang in the middle of Canada and right on the border with America. It was the coldest, gloomiest city I had ever visited. The unbelievable cold took effect as soon as we exited the airport. We had barely walked a couple of hundred metres to the carpark when it really hit us. Suddenly, I could not feel my fingers. During the drive around the city I noticed that there was barely any colour or plant life, only lifeless trees. The people seemed solemn and their faces could only just be seen behind their multi-layered clothing. I felt quite sorry for these people. There is no way I would consider this lifestyle to be *living*. I did not like the place at all. A heavy energy hung in the air; it gave me the creeps. I found everything about Winnipeg quite depressing. The hotel we stayed in was no better. It was flash, but there was something about it that made me uneasy. The building itself was unbelievably tall, the tallest I had ever stayed in. My room was on the fiftieth floor and when I parted the curtains, I found myself staring directly into clouds. I felt I could almost shake hands with God. I just stood there in silence, realising that I was all alone on the other side of the world without my family. I was both scared and elated at the same time. I could sense something around me – God or my old people or both, perhaps – acknowledging the unfolding of my journey throughout life. The spirits were with me at that moment; their presence in the hotel room as well as beyond was strong indeed.

I decided that I wasn't going to embrace Winnipeg and excused myself from all the planned outdoor trips except a visit to a club one night. Other than that I stayed indoors for the duration. I had no intention of investigating this cold, dark city, not at all. Instead I focused on my work and the reason why I was there.

My being rests contentedly
In my skin
Smelling the earth . . . consume
Everything in
I know this soil
That tree
That bird call
I knew it even a thousand years before
I walked
And slept
And ate
This earth
I talked with koorangan
Po
And twal
I remember paanj*'s bark*
And cambahl*'s snarl*
All sense wrapped together
As one
Just like cha ang . . .
Squashed
Liver and all
In paperbark
Baked back in earth
Tork, ndrangle *and* pri . . .
From country into me
Shaping a sense
Of identity
Bush grass sweet

Like honey on my tongue
The memories fresh
Like yesterday
Still smell that smell
Of smoke fire
On my hair
On my grandfather

Shortly after our arrival in Toronto we were driven out to Cape Croker, near Georgian Bay, 190 kilometres northwest. I absolutely loved it. Now this was something I had always imagined doing when I was younger and watched cowboy and Indian movies. I had always wanted to visit a Native Canadian or Native American reserve. The food, smells, community life and songs sat spiritually well with me. It was familiar stuff, regardless of how far I was from my own home. The opportunity to sing my granny's tribal song *Sara* to the people and then have an elder return the cultural exchange in song in turn was special indeed. I felt Nan with me in acknowledgement of the moment.

Fried scones and fish were cooked in almost exactly the same way we prepared these foods back home. I also tried pumpkin pie for the first time – not a favourite I soon discovered, though. I found it quite heavy. More singing and dancing followed the feasting and lasted into the evening. I could've stayed there all night listening to the spirits make themselves known through their descendants in this vast and truly magnificent land. This was awesome stuff.

Following the welcoming feast we made our way to the bed and breakfast that was to be home for us for the final week of our tour. Accommodation consisted of single and double cabins as well as the main house, which looked so warm and inviting that the representative from Victoria and I opted to stay there while the others chose the cabins a couple of hundred metres away. As the host led us girls up the stairs I was immediately drawn to the room to my left, which appeared to be the biggest. As soon as I entered, I immediately sensed a spirit present. It seemed to belong to a white female girl, in her teens or early twenties. She was quite thin in appearance and had long, straight, sandy-coloured hair. She wore a long, white nightgown with lace at the hem and buttons up the front and was looking straight at me. There were three beds in there, but the one that appealed to me the most was the large double bed in the centre of the room. A princess bed was what came to mind. The bedding was made of white lace and curtains draped around the bed and were secured by a golden canopy. It was quite high and I knew I'd have fun getting in and out of this very special bed. To the left of the princess bed was a single day bed, I placed my suitcase on it before heading downstairs to meet the others standing around the fire. Listening to the others sing, I stared up at the night sky. There was the moon, full, in all its glory staring back at me. For the first time since I arrived in Canada I realised the distance that separated me from my daughters Sheridan, Justice and Ebony.

The next morning I awoke to find myself not in the princess bed as I had intended, but on the day bed. Why I hadn't slept in the big bed I'm not sure, but something must have deterred me. The spiritual presence in the room remained. I remember feeling the thickness in the air as soon as I entered the room. I felt it as I lay staring into the darkness waiting for sleep to arrive. My last thought before succumbing to sleep was that I hoped nothing too freaky would happen. I'm pretty sure that bed once belonged to the girl and somehow she had kept me off it. On my way to the shower I lifted up the window and saw the magical sight of snow slowly drifting down. It was like I was in a movie, receiving blessing after blessing. We visited a beaver dam before dispersing and attending our respective workshops and presentations throughout the community. I was required to go with some of the other writers to the local schools to present some workshops. On arrival we were introduced to the staff and then directed to the primary section of the school. I treasured every single second I spent with my class and had a strong sense that I'd work with children again at some point in my life; it was just a matter of time.

I read some stories from both *Sandbeach Girl* and *Looking for Yams*, taught the kids some play songs that had been translated into my granny's language, Alngith, and did basic movement with the kids. One of the play songs we called *Waiee Waiee*, which basically translates to *Children Children* and is sung to the *Twinkle Twinkle Little Star* tune. During one of my readings a loud bang could be heard coming from just outside the window. One of the children ran to the window and looked outside.

'Miss, it's just a black bear raiding the bins.'

Oh my God, I truly was in Canada.

The afternoon before we were scheduled to fly back to Vancouver we all decided to go for a final walk, but when I looked outside something told me not to even try it. The land looked absolutely freezing. Nevertheless, I did not want to miss out on anything. I had already chickened out in Winnipeg and convinced myself that as long as I wrapped up I should be okay. I was wrong. About ten minutes into the walk I just stopped dead in my tracks. I couldn't walk, couldn't speak and it felt like pretty soon I wouldn't be able to breathe either. I felt that I was shutting down. Several of the others began rubbing my glove-covered hands and hugging me, but it was no use. While I still had life left in me I tracked it back to the safety of the house as fast as I possibly could.

Before too long we were tracking our way back across to Vancouver. It was Halloween and the flight crew were all decked out in costumes, keeping everyone on board entertained. That night we went out on the town for the last time before catching our flights back home. I must admit I felt a little spooked by all the gory costumes people were dressed in. By this stage I just wanted to get back home to my girls and family.

In Sydney I slept off the jet lag before hitting the city. I had decided to treat myself and get my hair done. Sitting in the departure lounge at Cairns airport the next day, I noticed a fella kept staring at me. A little while later he passed by me to go to the shops. We made eye contact and the biggest smile crossed both our faces.

'My sister, that you hey?'

We hugged. It was a brother of mine descending from Nan's brother's line.

'Well of course it's me, who else would it be?'

'You look different that's all,' he said, laughing. 'But it's your hair, it's made you look like them Indian mob.'

We laughed and hugged again.

The warmth of the North Queensland tropics sat on my skin, blanketing me. I was back on country.

Dick and Nyrlotte Kelinda with Jean George Awumpan (three years old), Aurukun, late 1920s

Fiona George at sixteen, Aboriginal and Islander Dance Theatre (AIDT), 1985

Fiona George with Lewis Lampton, 5th Year, NAISDA, Studio 1, 1990

Danny Doyle, Studio 1, NAISDA

Fiona George on her wedding day, 13 January 1990

Sheridan Nyrlotte, three months, Napranum, 1992

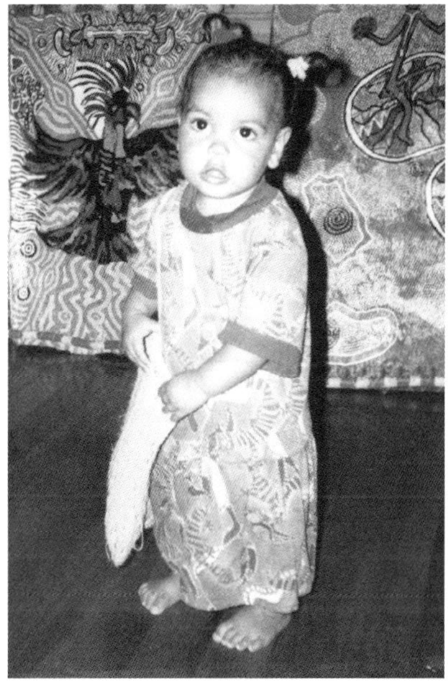

Justice Athailpun, two years old, Napranum, 1997

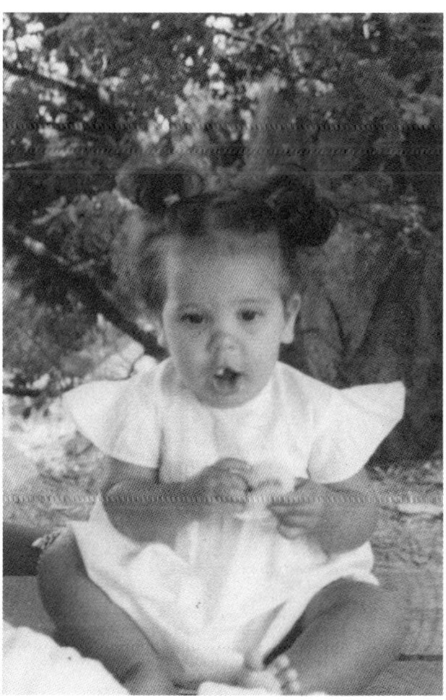

Ebony Anna Awumpan, Townsville, 2000

The girls with their maternal grandmother, Athailpun, early 2000s

Fiona and her Dad – their first meeting ever – Weipa airport, 1997

Fiona's Austrian great-grandparents

Fiona's paternal grandfather, Ferdinand Florian Wirrer

Fiona's paternal grandmother Anna Wirrer and her Dad on the family farm in Walz, Austria

'Snake Pot I', designed and painted by Fiona for her Dad, 1997

Awumpan (Fiona's maternal granny) and her Dad, holding Justice (aged two), at Napranum Rrutchuk Festival, 1997

Anna Wirrer, Fiona's paternal grandmother

Fiona doing *A Bastard's Tale*, a one-woman performance at Metro Arts during Shiela's Shorts, Magdalena Festival, Brisbane, 2002

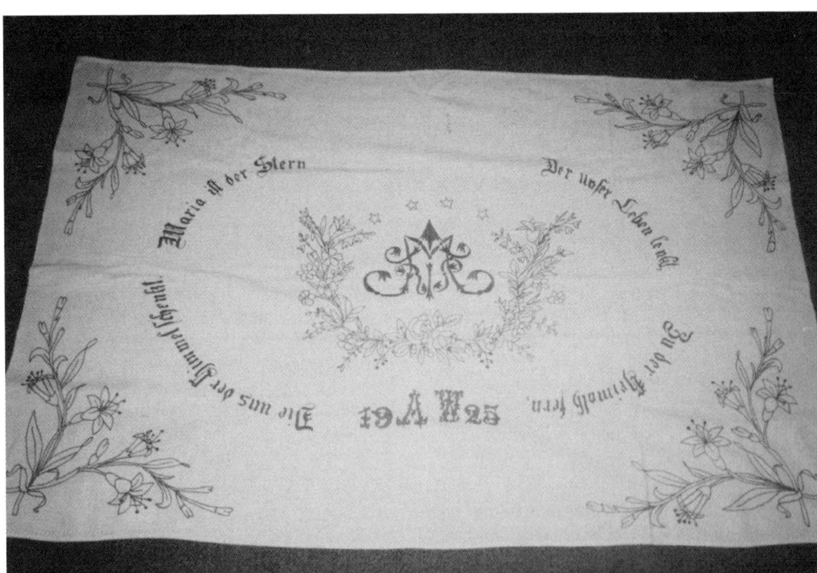

The cloth Fiona's Austrian grandmother, Anna, knitted with the family crest in 1925 (and passed on to Fiona)

Fiona dancing in Vancouver, Canada, during the Talking Stick Festival Tour, 2003

Fiona with school children at Cape Croker, Toronto, Canada, 2003

Fiona with Sue Abbey and Matt Foley at the presentation of the David Unaipon Award Ceremony, Brisbane Writer's Festival 2004

Stef Furlong, Fiona and Mum at Fiona's Graduation Ceremony, Cairns, 2003

CHAPTER SIXTEEN

I was home only for a week before I boarded a plane once more, this time with New Zealand as my destination. It ached me to do this to Danny and the girls so soon after the Canada trip, but this holiday had been something us girls who were studying together at RATEP had planned earlier that year. We'd been fundraising and preparing for months, so there was no way I could've pulled out from the much-needed holiday us girls felt we had earned after all our hard work studying. We had become a group that was supportive of each other.

'Mummy, why you have to go away again?' asked Justice one day. She had removed her thumb from her mouth especially to present this question to me.

'Because it's something that my group at uni decided to do a while ago, bubba.'

'Yeah but why do you have to go? Do you have to leave us?'

Back in the mouth went her little thumb as she awaited my

response. That question hurt my heart, as did looking into those gorgeous, big eyes.

'Bubba, it's not for too long this time. It's only for half the time the Canada trip took. Would you like Mummy to buy you something? How 'bout a tiki?'

She stopped sucking her thumb briefly. 'What's a tiki?'

'Well, it's a traditional Maori symbol. You could wear it as a necklace if you want.' No response, just those huge, dark cherry eyes staring back at me, through me, melting my chest area. 'You know,' I continued, kneeling beside her and placing my hands on her shoulders, 'when I was about your age your sissy, my nan, went to New Zealand and brought me back a tiki. I thought I was real deadly with that thing. Now I can bring one back for you, what you reckon?'

She shrugged. 'Yeah okay then.'

Once more there was Danny with our three girls draped off him at the Weipa Airport waving goodbye to me.

Seven of us plus our two tutors, Carrie Gay and Rowena Wallace, landed at Auckland Airport and picked up two vehicles that would transport us around the North Island. Compared to Canada, I knew this trip would be more laidback and, as much as I missed my girls, I allowed myself to enjoy the experience. We were invited to a *Powhiri* or Welcome Ceremony, done to ward off evil spirits and unite both visitor and host in an environment of friendship and peace. Once more, my spirit became fat from the experience. After we were slowly sung to, we were invited to enter the main house and find a place on a mattress on the floor.

I looked around the space and noticed hundreds of photos lining the walls.

'Who are these people?' I whispered to the person next to me.

'These are the faces of our ancestors and our families who have passed on.'

Wow, I thought to myself. This was serious stuff. We had been welcomed into a very special space indeed.

Once everyone was seated we were prompted to introduce ourselves and speak briefly about where we were from, adding anything that we considered significant. I introduced myself as a Wik descendant from the Western Cape and expressed how incredibly humbled I felt to be invited into the Marai – the Marai is a place of special spiritual significance to the Maori. Naturally I sensed the spirits of the ancestors around the room. How fortunate I was to be experiencing such things.

Before we headed back home us girls decided to hit the town in Hamilton. Of all places to party, we decided to check out the red light district. There was never a dull moment with the RATEP gang of 2002.

My brain adapted easily to the intellectual challenges of studying again and I especially loved the assignments – although I didn't enjoy teleconference time, which was the primary means of participating in lectures given by our tutors. I loved working at my own pace on the computer and interacting and exchanging electronically, though. I discovered I still wasn't friends with maths all these years later, but figured if I was going to be teaching the stuff I had to at least develop an interest in it.

My days were long and demanding. I was surviving on about three to four hours sleep to get assignments in on time as well as pass exams. Danny never complained that I was so busy all the time. He took one step at a time juggling his twelve-hour shifts driving trucks with helping out with the girls and housework. Likewise, the girls never complained. Life was busy for all of us. However, the regular trips flying out to Townsville for up to two weeks at a time began to prove difficult for me. I especially missed Ebony as she was still quite little. And I found Townsville an unpleasant city; the majority of people presented themselves as ignorant and having stereotypical ideas about Indigenous people in general. Comments were made to me about my own people as if I, myself, wasn't Aboriginal. I found this confusing, as I still do today. Whitefellas will say things like, 'Aborigines used to be nomadic didn't they?' And I'd think why this person was talking about 'Aborigines' as if I wasn't one.

On one occasion following a fairly enjoyable conversation, a taxi driver farewelled me with, 'You're not like the blacks around here, you appear to be fairly smart in comparison. Where did you go to school?'

I didn't know what to say. I was so shocked I just looked at him for a second or two then, without saying a word, slowly shut the door and walked away.

My first practical teaching experience had me at the Western Cape College, known back then as the Weipa North State School. I really believed that I wouldn't have any problems at this school, well at least not socially. I was wrong. I found the energy and attitudes in the staffroom stand-offish and unsupportive. The first day I thought that maybe the staff needed an icebreaker or something and then surely they'd soon start talking. But the second day the behaviour was repeated. It upset me a little, but I kept telling myself that it wasn't personal and things would settle. But this behaviour lasted right throughout that first week. I just gave up and hung out in my classroom or in the playground. My daughters attended this school, we lived across the road and this was not only my hometown historically, but traditionally as well. Yet, here I was being made to feel like a total outcast. I found it odd that so-called professional people treated others in this way, especially in an environment where the adults were supposedly the ones responsible for nurturing and cultivating attitudes and beliefs that were inclusive and respectful of all.

Regardless of that negative experience, my supervising teacher was excellent – Year 1 had a very experienced, laidback teacher. She knew her craft and respectfully shared her wealth of knowledge and skills with me. I was relieved when I realised that this teacher had no hang-ups that would interfere with what I was there for. Her calm approach and manner immediately settled me. I remember the very first time I was to lead a session. A group of twenty or so five-year-olds sat quietly in their chairs staring at me. Oh my God, what have I gotten myself into? was my first thought. They were cute, but scary. What was I supposed to do with so many of them? I was flat out keeping my own girls busy and interested. Once the nerves settled instinct mixed with theory kicked in though and the rest just takes care of itself. I loved the class I had been given, as well as the whole teaching experience overall.

Second-year prac had me fly out to Townsville once more to a Year 1 class at Belgium Gardens Primary School, at the foot of Castle Hill. The staff were a little more friendly compared to back in Weipa. I did notice looks of curiosity on the faces of some of the parents though and was gently warned by my supervising teacher, who was great, that some of the parents might find it 'interesting' that the teacher of their children was Aboriginal. Her warning made me want to deliver the best I could; it worked for me as opposed to against me. By the end of my five-week block I had those students singing, dancing and speaking in my granny's language.

Fortunately, my final prac was done at the Napranum school campus where I had a composite class of Years 5, 6 and 7. I absolutely loved it, particularly switching from lower primary to upper primary and making the necessary adjustments to the delivery of content. I experimented even more with ensuring my teaching approach was culturally appropriate. I based my lesson plans and delivery on the New Basics approach and found the strategies and planning interesting. For these students, maths would be covered by, say, looking for a didgeridoo and estimating the length of a tree that would be suitable to make the instrument. Science would be covered by surveying the land and its flora and fauna. What makes a certain part of the bush good didge country? Why are the trees hollow? Art would be covered through the painting or talking about the significance of particular designs and symbols, how patterns and colours work together. We identified the traditional custodians of that part of country and would get permission as well as display our respects and acknowledgement of the identified nation, and so on – that would obviously take care of studies of societies and environment (SOSE). Music was covered by inviting a community member to come in to give the boys lessons in didge playing, and because the didgeridoo was not traditionally an instrument of the Cape this was made known to the students. The girls would be responsible for designing and creating posters on the computer to advertise didge performance and raffling off the didge on the day. Once more I had an excellent prac supervisor who basically trusted what I was doing.

The classroom I was in during this prac was the same one where I saw my Year 2 teacher and a male teacher making out, way back in the mid seventies. I remember thinking that was what all teachers got up to the end of the school day. Now here I was playing the role of teacher. I looked toward the window, reflecting that, overall, my generation of Indigenous teachers in training would never really be seen to quite measure up to the know-it-all non-Indigenous educators. It was not my imagination, I did not go digging for negatives and I am not making mountains out of molehills. I experienced enough conversations and scenarios as a student teacher to justify my opinion that this was the case. Even teacher aides or educational helpers displayed such attitudes. It made my blood boil, but on the other hand their self-indulgent ignorance fuelled my desire to remain focused and to continue to aspire.

Although initially I'd set out to acquire skills in early childhood education, here I was three years later with a degree in the primary sector. I had graduated as an S1 graduate – the highest level you could graduate at. What was I going to do with this qualification? My love for the arts, including performance, was as strong as ever and my journey into the world of print only just beginning to unfold. Deep down I knew that I was not at all ready to teach.

CHAPTER SEVENTEEN

Throughout my tertiary studies, my ongoing dabbling in the performing arts enabled me to keep choreographing for local schools, particularly during Croc Eisteddfod time, as well as choreographing for the two communities of Weipa and Napranum in general. This connection with dance was essential for my creative spirit – it fed it and kept it breathing. Fortunately, my beautiful little family just accepted that side of me. They knew that dance was my other family, my other marriage, as corny as that may sound. There were never any complaints or resistance from Dan or the girls. The understanding was that if Mum had to do something or be somewhere then our family life and routine just adjusted itself to make it happen.

In October 2000, Dan and I were invited to take a performing group down to Canberra for the Trackin *Kultja* Festival. We informed Dad and, as usual, it was decided that he'd travel from Gosford by car and meet us there. Dan and I packed our eight-seater van with the girls and my nieces and drove overland to Cairns. Novotel sponsored half the trip and put us up in their hotels both in Port Douglas and Canberra in exchange for a performance in one of their restaurants before we were scheduled to fly out.

Canberra was a good opportunity to catch up with artists from other parts of Australia and witness firsthand what and how creativity was being practised in the performing and visual arts arena. It was especially fantastic for my girls and nieces to be a part of it all, as both performers and spectators. Unfortunately, Dad missed our performance, and to this day I regret not stalling and waiting for him. He arrived not long after we finished performing. We had just walked off stage when I noticed him burst in through the museum doors.

'Dad, where were you?'

'I was having a yarn with George, Princess, I hope I haven't missed the performance.'

'We just finished the second one –' I stopped mid-speech. 'Uhm, George who?'

'You know George.'

I stared at him blankly.

'You know from Warumpi Band.'

'Oh.' I found it quite funny. Was I supposed to know George? 'That George, of course,' I nodded with a smile.

We decided to go shopping once we were done checking out the other performances.

Dan and Rhonda Parry, one of the other artists in our performing group, took Sheridan, Justice and my twin nieces Jonyelle and Bridgette in one direction while Dad, Ebony and I went in another. As we strolled through the shops Dad carried Ebony on his shoulders.

'Princess, I want you to know that I have included Ebony in the will.' He paused before continuing. 'So when the time comes, then you and the girls will get your share.'

I didn't respond. I had always felt slightly uncomfortable discussing topics of a financial nature with Dad as I felt that this was what his wife had accused me of. Besides, he had mentioned business about his will several times already, before Ebony was born.

'Fiona, did you hear me?'

'Yes, I heard you, Dad.'

'Good, well that's settled then.'

I noticed Dad had begun to tire, so I suggested we go back to the hotel so that both he and Ebony could relax and get some rest. As we sat and chatted over a cuppa I could tell Dad had something on his mind. He had Ebony firmly plonked on his lap. The whole time she just sat there quietly and stared at him.

'Princess, I've had some tests done.'

I knew it. This was what I'd been sensing when we first entered the room. Dad had seemed a little distant and edgy.

'It's nothing serious, but they have found something and are in the process of working out exactly what it is.'

'How are you feeling, Dad?'

'Great, my girl, I feel great. Just a little tired from time to time that's all.'

'Please look after yourself.'

'I will.'

'And please let me know as soon as you know what's going on, yeah?'

'I will.'

We spent several days in Canberra together before Dad had to track back to Gosford. The morning he was scheduled to leave, Dan, the girls and I waited out the front of the hotel. Dad pulled up out the front and got out of his car. He quietly hugged Sheridan, then Justice, then Ebony. He shook Danny's hand and then hugged me for a long time.

'See ya, mate,' he said.

Before joining the flow of traffic he looked at me one more time. The feeling that came through his eyes engulfed me. Through tears I watched him drive off and disappear.

'Mum, why are you crying? We'll see grandad again,' Justice announced soothingly.

She was such a sensitive and considerate girl.

Not long after that we saw Rhonda and the twins off at the airport as they were flying back home while we drove overland. I absolutely love travelling by road and getting to see country on the ground, especially with my family. As we farewelled the bitumen road and skidded onto the familiar dirt that would carry us homeward, I looked back at our three beautiful daughters stretched out across the van. I loved these moments when it was just Dan and me and our little family travelling the land together. I knew this country; from Laura onwards this all spelled home to me. I smiled to myself as I realised that my girls would develop a relationship with the land as they travelled it. They would grow accustomed to the bushland that guided us along, the smells and sounds that would sing us closer to the Cape. Justice and Ebony appeared to be the most observant of the three of them, always watching and listening intently. I wondered what was going on in their little minds.

After some time on the road, the land began to appear

unfamiliar. We've always had red dirt, but this particular dirt was different; the red was more a burnt orange colour and the texture was smoother, not so pebble riddled.

'Danny, this place don't look right. This doesn't look like the way home.'

'Aah, we right,' was his response as he stubbornly kept driving.

A small whirlwind danced in the centre of the road and then skipped off into the bush. I felt an overwhelming sadness and immediately thought that perhaps there was something wrong with Nan, maybe she wasn't well. I also began to sense an odd energy around us. No-one was talking and it was eerily silent outside the vehicle as well. The girls were unusually quiet. The energy was so strong I began to cry.

'What you crying for, Mum?' asked one of the girls.

'I don't know, something's not right.'

'Where?'

'I don't know, I just know something serious is going to happen soon,' I explained.

The girls remained silent.

Up ahead I noticed something standing in the middle of the road. As we came closer I cautioned Danny to slow down.

'Look there,' I whispered.

'Let's get him,' replied Danny, always wanting to pursue wildlife.

'No, leave him. This is a bit freaky, he could be story one.'

The van came to a halt. The dingo stood there looking at us as we returned the stare. And then, just like that, it ran off into the bush.

'You're on the wrong track. Turn around and back track.'

An hour or so we later we were back at where Danny had taken the wrong turn. If we had kept going we would've ended up on the East coast, directly opposite where we were heading.

Life pretty much continued as per usual following our Trackin *Kultja* Festival trip. The older kids were back at school for the final quarter of the year, I was back at uni and Ebony was back with her babysitter.

One day during the Christmas break I answered the phone to Dad's daily call. I was feeling pretty good about everything. It had been a full year, busy but productive. Besides, I loved this time of year. Shopping for presents, decorating the tree with the girls, the rain, the rotten mangoes, everything about Christmas time in the Cape soothed my spirit.

'It's cancer.'

Pause.

'What? What do you mean?' was all I could manage.

'It's all those smokes I've had, the damage has been done.'

'So what does this mean now, Dad?'

'Well the good news is that the doctors say I have a good chance of beating it.'

Silence.

'Don't worry, Princess, it will be fine. I feel great. Chemo will begin next week, it will all work out.'

Pause. 'Do you want me to do anything? Is there anything I can do?'

'No. There's absolutely nothing to worry about. Just do me a favour and tell Sheridan for me, will you do that?'

'Of course I will.'

Sheridan was playing in the backyard. I called her over.

'Sheri, come and sit down bub. I spoke to Grandad and there's something he wants me to tell you.'

She looked at me.

'Do you know what cancer is?'

She nodded. 'Is Grandad alright?'

'Yes, he is, but the doctors found some abnormal cells. He's got cancer, he wanted me to tell you, okay?'

She nodded, turned around and went about her business.

'Sheridan,' I called out.

She stopped and turned to me.

'You okay?'

'Yep.'

'You sure?' I walked up to her. 'What are you thinking?'

'Nothing, Mum. I'm just gonna pray for him, that's all.'

Dad asked about her the following day.

'She said she'll pray for you.'

Silence. Dad had made no secret of being an atheist. He much preferred the evolution theory of how we came to be and where we will supposedly end up. I recalled a conversation Dad and I had had previously regarding my belief in God.

'It is religion that is responsible for war.' His voice travelled down the phone that day.

'Yes, Dad but our faith is in the Lord Jesus and that is not being religious. That is Christianity. The religious people of the day judged Jesus and crucified him, declaring that he was guilty of blasphemy and sin.' And on and on it would go.

I snapped back to reality.

'Are you okay with that?' I asked, remembering how stubborn he could get with this kind of talk.

'Tell Sheridan her grandad would like that very much.'

CHAPTER EIGHTEEN

About a week later Dad called again. As soon as we got talking I noticed that he wasn't as articulate as he normally was. His sentences seemed to be incomplete and slightly scatty and there appeared to be some slurring in his pronunciation.

'Dad, are you okay? Should I come down, do you want me to fly down?'

'It's just the chemotherapy. I will be fine, I don't want you to waste your money, Princess.'

'Okay, but you keep me informed? I need to know to be aware of what's happening to you and what you're going through.'

'Yes, I will let you know.'

Several days later Dad called again, but this time he could barely speak at all. I was doing all the talking. The slurring was even worse and Dad wasn't making any sense at all.

'Put Gretal on Dad. I want to speak to her.'

'What?' she snapped.

'I just want to know what's happening to Dad. He's not sounding too good.'

'Well, what do you expect, Fiona. What do you want me to say?'

'I want to fly down to see him.'

'And do what?'

'Just be with him, or be there for him.'

'Look, there's no point in doing that.'

'Never mind, put Dad back on. I want to say goodbye to him.'

That night, before we called it a day, I gathered the girls. 'What are we doing?' they asked as we sat in a circle and held hands.

'We're praying for Grandad.'

'Please Lord Jesus, do what's best for Grandad and may your will be done in his life. Amen.'

That night as I fell off to sleep I decided to book a flight down to Sydney first thing in the morning.

The phone woke me. I wasn't sure where the girls were but Dan and I were still in bed. It was about 9 am on 13 January 2002.

'Can you get that, Dan?' I asked, nudging him out of bed.

'It's for you,' echoed his voice down the hallway.

I had been restless all night and now ran to the lounge room. The girls were watching cartoons on TV while eating their cereal.

'It's that mob,' Dan whispered as he passed the phone to me.

'Hello.'

'Fiona, Fred's dead. He passed away this morning. He woke up, went to have breakfast, sat at the kitchen bench and just fell backwards. It was very quick.'

'No.' I started to sob quietly.

'I'm sorry, Fiona.' And with that she hung up.

I looked at my daughters, unaware, continuing to eat their breakfast and occasionally laugh at whatever it was they were watching. I looked over at Danny.

'Dad's gone,' I whispered.

Dan walked over and held me quietly for a long time.

It was as if I was stuck in a bad dream. I could not function. I waited for my daily phone call from Dad telling me that they were just playing tricks with me and that he was fine. I curled up in bed waiting. I cried constantly for the remainder of the day. I'm not sure how Nan and Mum heard the news, but later that day Mum visited us. Lyn must've brought her in.

'Oh no, Fay, I am so sorry,' is all I remember her saying as she quietly shed tears for the man who briefly crossed paths with her so long ago.

The next morning, Dan rang and enquired about the funeral. They informed him it was going to be in a couple of days. It would be difficult for us to make the trip from the Cape to Gosford on time.

'Don't worry, babe,' said Dan reassuringly. 'I'll sort it out with work and see how much we got in our travel account.'

I'm not sure how long I remained in bed. The kids went about their business as Danny arranged everything. I sobbed into my pillow.

We're all sitting around a table. I'm not sure who else is at the table, but Dad is there, sitting to my right. See, I tell myself,

I was right all along. Dad's not dead. I decide to go over to him. I tap him on the head from behind and his head dangles loosely to the side. He appears to be in deep sleep. I walk around to face him and nudge him on the shoulder so as to wake him up, but my hands protrude into his skin and flesh.

I woke up in the middle of the night covered in sweat. I could hear Danny snoring as a gecko called out above my head.

'We leaving in the morning, babe, pack your stuff. Girls are packing theirs and I'll do Ebony's. Work got us covered and I'm taking compassionate leave. It's all in the bag.'

I didn't want to get out of bed.

'Babe?'

'What?'

'Have a shower, come on.' He sat beside me and placed his hand on mine gently. 'You'll feel better if you shower. We have a plane to catch.' I did as was told.

We got to Sydney and stayed overnight in a hotel before catching the train out to Gosford the next day. I was curled up in the foetal position all night and I couldn't stop crying. I just wanted to hear my father's voice. I must've woken Danny up.

'You right, babe?'

I kept sobbing. He knew what to do. He gently hinted to me to mix spirits. I didn't resist. We made love.

'I need to see Dad,' I said to Danny when we arrived in Gosford. So after checking into our hotel Danny rang the crematorium. He placed the receiver down quietly.

'Well? When can we go?'

'No-one's allowed to view him.'

'But surely that doesn't include me. I'm his daughter.'

'They sounded pretty strong about it. I think they mean especially you.'

I sensed that Danny knew more than he was prepared to reveal to me. He was trying so hard to be gentle, but it was obvious that I was going to be treated as an outcast from here on. I was too weak and emotionally numb to react. As confused as I was, I just let it go and decided to save what little emotional energy I had for the funeral service. I simply could not do anything. I could not think, feel or speak. I felt like all my energy had been sucked out of me and I was just existing in a slow motion dream. I wanted to wake up and realise that it was just a horrible nightmare.

By the time we arrived at the service the place was pretty much packed. A large photo of Dad smiling was at the entry into the building. On it were the words *Ferdinand 'Fred' Wirrer 1938–2002*. I found myself still hoping that soon someone was going to tell me that there had been a huge mistake and that, in fact, Dad was fine. Still, I continued on as if I was on autopilot.

As we entered the chapel I immediately noticed the majority of Gretal's family were seated to the right. People stood all along the back as seats were limited. I spotted some empty seats three rows from the front on the left-hand side.

I visualise my dad in the coffin in front of me.

I tuned into the service. The minister talked about Dad's life, his wife, his family at Gosford, his friends. She read out poems written by the little girls who lived just up the road and then placed the poems and other tributes on Dad's coffin.

There was no mention of me, of his blood granddaughters. Nothing, not a hint. It was almost as if by not acknowledging us it would make us go away, just disappear, as if we didn't exist. They did not even so much as look in our direction. There was no greeting, no acknowledgement, no welcome.

As the service came to an end the curtains opened and Dad's coffin slowly retreated. Andrea Bocelli's *Time to Say Goodbye* played in the background.

The thought of what was once my father soon being reduced to ashes freaks me to the core.

I began to shake, struggling to breathe. Sobs invaded my chest cavity. Everyone else left the building except for me. I allowed myself to mourn the only way I know how.

After a while someone placed her hand on my shoulder.

'Excuse me ma'am, but you're going to have to leave soon.'

I ignored her and stayed where I needed to be.

'Ma'am.'

I looked up.

'Have you people got no heart? That is my blood in there, no-one else's, but mine. I will leave when I am ready!'

She walked away and joined Fred's 'family', leaving me to my business.

I left the building when I was ready to and noticed the group of men that had been standing up the back still on the veranda. As soon as I walked toward them they approached me.

One of them extended his hand toward me.

'Hello, I was a friend of your father. Your father talked about you all the time. He loved you very much. I'm very pleased to meet you.'

I shook his hand. The others followed suit. There were a number of them, probably about five or six.

'Don't worry about that woman!' The last man had a strong accent. 'Your father was a good friend to me. Don't worry about them,' he continued, nodding toward Gretal and family. 'That woman my friend was married to is a very bossy woman. Always wants things to be done her way.'

'Are you going to the wake?' asked another.

'I don't think I'll be welcome,' I responded.

'Don't worry. You and your family are welcome to come to my house. How are you getting back to Sydney?'

'We're not sure yet. We haven't planned that far ahead.'

'Well it's sorted then. You come with me, I have plenty of room in my van, see?' He pointed to his eight-seater van.

I felt a tap on my back.

'Excuse me, ma'am, but I thought you would like this.' The service attendant handed me a red carnation. 'I got it off the coffin.'

I hugged him.

'Thank you. Thank you so very much.'

On the way back to Sydney our new Turkish friend phoned his wife. They conversed in their language before he turned to us.

'All done. We shall have a small feast at my house in memory of Fred.'

Once back home I asked Dan to call Dad's wife and request some of his ashes for my keepsake.

'She seems to like you. Hopefully she'll cooperate and find it in her heart to be considerate for once.'

Dan made the call. It appeared to have gone well.

'Well, what did she say?'

'Yep, she'll do it when she's ready.'

To this day I have not received anything.

part 3
Changing Heart

CHAPTER NINETEEN

In 2002, the mentor that the David Unaipon judges requested I work with, Melissa Lucashenko, arrived to spend some time familiarising herself with me, Nan, my extended family and country to hopefully gain a better understanding of the spirit behind my manuscript *Whispers of This Wik Woman*. The version that had been awarded a highly commended needed more work in order for it to reach a broader audience. I wanted to share Nan's story, but needed guidance. We spent the better part of a week yarning and visiting places, and basically just raking through the story slowly in order for me to rewrite the manuscript. Melissa noticed my inability to focus. I kept talking about Dad and his death and everything related to it.

'Fiona, we can't get into *Whispers* unless you empty what's preoccupying you about your dad's passing.'

I looked at her.

'Get some butcher's paper and a couple of coloured markers.'

I did as I was instructed.

'Spread it out on the floor and write down anything and everything that comes to mind.'

Sometime later I looked back at the trail of paper strewn across the lounge room floor. There, in scattered print form, lay a story waiting to be told. Satisfied with the process, I folded the pieces of paper up and put them away until the time came when I would have to refer to them. I was now ready to work through the mentoring process with Melissa in order to get *Whispers* ready for submission.

The whole process took just under a year, but was worth every second of it. Somehow I managed to complete the revised manuscript alongside my studies for uni. Where I found the time to do both I don't know. The phone call from Sue Abbey at University of Queensland Press (UQP) was a moment that I had been waiting to inhale for some time.

'Fiona, you did it. You've got the top award.'

Phew! Was all I could think. How did I get there?

Sweet Jesus has sure been good to me.

After that day where I spider-mapped where I was at emotionally and mentally following Dad's death, I occasionally looked at the sheets of butcher's paper I had tucked away in my cupboard. I did not know what to do with the range of issues that continued to live inside of me. And I was having bizarre dreams about Dad.

He appears out the front of our place and is calling out to me.

'Bout time he turns up, I say to myself as I rush out to

the front. I realise he wants to tell me something. He begins to speak, but as he does so his image starts to fade and becomes transparent. He is speaking and is trying to tell me something, but I can't seem to hear him, I cannot make sense of what is coming out of his mouth. I begin to panic so I go to hug him, to beg him to remain with me and not leave me again. As I do so my hands slip through the image as if it is a hologram. The image of Dad slowly disintegrates before me. He is gone again. Damn it! I say to myself. Why does he keep leaving me?

I still wasn't dealing with Dad's passing at all. I didn't know how to. It had been almost a year since he left and, yet, not a day went by without me hearing his voice, or seeing him or finding myself waiting for the phone to ring expecting it to be him. One day I grabbed everything he'd given me, everything except my granny's cloth, and took them outside to burn. I wanted to burn him, get rid of all evidence of him ever entering my life in the first place.

My daughters stopped me and saved all they could, hiding things in secret places where I couldn't find them.

'Don't burn these, Mum,' Sheridan said sternly as she and Justice quickly rescued whatever they could. 'These are special memories of Grandad.'

A couple of weeks later I noticed a special-looking letter among the usual pile of bills in our mailbox. The envelope was very soft and a pale blue colour. I didn't open it until I got home.

I got comfortable in the backyard. I knew this letter had something to do with Dad. It was from Austria and written by my cousin Andrea. She introduced herself to me and went on to tell me that she'd had a dream about me. She dreamed I was in pain, so she and the rest of the family wanted me to know that they were thinking of me and loved me.

I spun out as I calculated that the time she'd had the dream was around about the same time I had wanted to burn everything that connected me to Austria and my Wirrer bloodline. Oh my God. Could it be that she felt my spirit all the way over there, even though I had not even met her yet? The letter confirmed to me that Dad's death was not the end of my journey of self-discovery and identity searching. It was only the beginning.

That same year I received a phone call from a theatre group known as deBASE Productions, which was based in Brisbane. I was immediately interested.

'We were told that you may have some work to present during the Sheila's Shorts Festival to be held here in Brisbane which will coincide with the Magdalena International Festival for Women. Would you be interested in participating?'

I had never really written for stage apart from the time I'd written *Television Stories*, which was worked into a dramatic piece and performed during the *Kayn Walu* end-of-year production during my fourth year at Naisda. But I really wanted this opportunity. So I decided to tell a little fib just to get a foot in the door.

'Of course I would be interested. In fact I have something basically ready to go.'

'That's great,' said the voice on the other end of the line. 'Would you be able to send us something so that we could, you know, get an idea of what it's about?'

Crap!

'Yep, no worries, is the end of the week okay?'

'That'll be fine, looking forward to it.'

What had I done? All I had was a belly full of emotions. I had to think of something real fast. Lucky for me I had bought some plays from a second-hand shop while in Cairns with Melissa regarding business surrounding *Whispers*.

These books turned out to be very helpful. I got an idea of how to structure a play after scrolling through *Pygmalion* by George Bernard Shaw, *Three More Plays* by Sean O'Casey and *Statements* by Athol Fugard. I convinced myself I could write a play, no worries. I had a story to tell and I wanted to act and dance it. *A Bastard's Tale* was my chosen title, as I worked through structuring the yarn onto paper. This story practically leapt out of me. I knew that, although drama was the dominant genre in this piece, dance was going to also be a big part of my expression. I kept referring to the butcher's paper. It really helped.

Before I knew it I was off to Brisbane to work with my director and then to rehearse the play. I had two weeks to do that and another week scheduled for performances. I had gone from no acting to preparing and presenting a fifty-minute long, one-woman show. What was I thinking?

Nan, Mum, Aunty Fran, Dan and the girls all travelled down for its debut. By that stage Nan's mind had begun to become very forgetful at times. She was really getting on in years, but, fortunately, was still able to make the trip down to Brisbane. Being a jetsetter in her earlier years, she loved travelling and I'm sure she felt really deadly getting on that plane.

A Bastard's Tale was intended to portray my conception, my childhood, my initial encounter with the term 'bastard' and my decision to analyse my identity. It depicted the journey lived in terms of looking for and finding my father through to his death, which opened up my journey to Austria and connecting with families over there and beyond. It ended with my finding closure in terms of self-identification and acceptance. There was a part in the play where I re-enacted Nan looking for Mum, as Mum had just returned from being out with my father behind her parents' backs.

'Annie, where you bin? Where you bin, Annie? You bin with that white man, hey?' was my line.

Suddenly Nan turned around and started asking Mum the same question once more. Talk about the biggest distraction! Mum cringed and the girls and I didn't know what to think. Thankfully, though, the audience found it entertaining.

Toward the end of that week I was having lunch with a group of other artists at the Powerhouse when a girl sporting the biggest grin made her way over to me.

'Excuse me, my name is Leticia Cáceres and I just wanted to tell you I saw your play last night and loved it very much. I'm with the Queensland Theatre Company and would love you to audition for an upcoming play that I will be directing. Please give me a call if you're interested.'

She handed her card to me.

'Uhm, I'm leaving in a couple of days, I don't think I'll be able to audition.'

'Then when can you make it? If we have to, we'll make the time for you before you leave.' She reached into her bag and pulled out a script. 'Read over this and let us know if you would be interested in auditioning at a time that suits you.'

That night I read through the script and even though I thought it was a little strange I was interested in the process that would take place in order to get it to stage, even though it would've meant leaving the family again if my audition were to be successful. Next thing I knew I was in front of Leticia, the writer and a representative from QTC presenting monologues and answering questions.

Being a part of this play required me to leave home for nine weeks. How on earth was I going to cope with two-and-a-half months away from my daughters? I rented a self-contained apartment on Montague Road, just down the road from the theatre in South Brisbane, and basically just got on with it. When I wasn't in rehearsals or learning lines or catching up with sleep I was painting. I bought a canvas and some paint and decided to depict my visual interpretation of the play.

The crew involved in the project were great and the cast were excellent. Not for one second was I ever made to feel different or inferior in any way. I suppose I was sort of expecting to be treated differently because I wasn't a 'trained' actor as such and was inexperienced in the art form. But it wasn't like that at all. I was so comfortable working with this group of people.

Regardless of the enjoyable creative process, I became extremely lonely and really missed my family. It felt like I was lost or, worse still, dead and couldn't make it back to where my family was. Still I wanted to experience being part of this play, regardless of the cost to me and my family. I knew my girls were with their father, their friends and our extended families and that they, too, would grow from this experience.

Five weeks later we were on stage in the Bille Brown Studio. I was fortunate to have Mum in the audience one night, as she had been in town for a church meeting and was able to make time to attend.

'Bubba, I really don't like how they put you in that box. You're not a dog.'

'Mum, it's not intentional, we're telling a story remember?'

'Yeah, but I still don't like, not one bit.' Mum went on and on about it.

By the time Dan arrived for the final show I could barely recognise him. It was almost like looking into the face of a stranger. Yet this was my husband. I had missed him so much. I loved him being with me.

I had done it. Nine weeks away from the girls and I had completed an excellent – though challenging – creative process that could only add to my journey through the performing arts.

CHAPTER TWENTY

Following the big break away I settled back into life, what with wrapping the year up and preparing for Christmas. During my time in Brisbane I'd kept thinking how convenient it would be if the whole family moved back down there together and made it our base. I was tired of plane travel and particularly of leaving the girls behind all the time. Brisbane seemed to be where doors kept opening for me now that I had gained some exposure as an artist again. Dan and I found ourselves entertaining the possibility of relocating. Both of us were reluctant as Weipa offered almost everything we required to bring up our young family. We had a four-bedroom place where rent was automatically deducted from Dan's wages, so we didn't even notice it at all. Dan was in a pretty secure employment situation. The girls were settled with friends, school was across the road, families were just at Naps, we lived on country – the list of benefits went on. Why would we want to leave all this behind? I resented the fact that I was even considering it. Nan was getting on, her mind becoming much more feeble. If there was ever a time she needed me it was now.

Regardless, I felt that I could no longer remain in Weipa and Dan seemed to agree with me. The tug to test the stage and what the arts might still have to offer me was strong. Just as I had done way back at eighteen, Dan and I drew up a list of positives and negatives. We came to the decision to pursue life in the city.

Dan resigned from work and 1 January 2004 was booked as our travel date. That morning, Lyn and Bob put on a breakfast barbeque at their place at Naps to farewell us. Pulling up at the front of the house and seeing Nan sitting under the shed at the back on her own made me ache so much. I don't think she fully understood that we were leaving. In a way, though, I was grateful that she didn't.

We had a great time that morning with family. For the first time no fights erupted, thanks to the absence of alcohol. Before we left, all Nan's great-grandchildren lined up and sang a song for her. She sat there with tears rolling down her cheeks.

Several hours later the plane lifted leaving my home behind. I looked back down at country, at the rivers leading out to the open sea, the red dirt that continues to be raped by machinery, the towns of Weipa and Naps. I felt sad about what I was doing to my daughters. As a result of what I was doing they may never know this place – this land – in quite the same way as I do.

Our budget allowed us up to three weeks to find a place to move into. In the meantime we stayed in an apartment. For some reason I was sending Danny into the real estate agents to submit our applications. I felt that my looks were a bit more pronounced and would limit our chances of getting approval given the assumptions made about renting to Aboriginal people. I felt that Dan had a bit more of a chance. Don't ask me to explain why I felt this way, shamefully I just did. In no time, though, we got a place in Capalaba, which was good as Dan had relatives living out there so the girls would be close to family on their father's side. The house was right at the end of a cul-de-sac that backed onto a park. Koalas lived in the trees; the girls labelled them killer koalas on account of the grunting sounds they made at night. They hadn't heard anything like it.

About a week later our belongings and furniture arrived from Weipa and I immediately set the place up so the girls could get settled. We enrolled them at Capalaba State College with Sheridan entering Year 7, Justice in Year 4 and Ebony commencing Prep. Danny had three months pay up his sleeve, so this provided an income while we got stuck into looking for work. We also had a fair amount in savings as backup.

I got my CV together and paid the Arts Council a visit, informing them that I was new in town and looking for work in acting. Within the week I received a phone call informing me of auditions in Lismore for a play titled *The Flood*, written by Janis Balodis. I got the part. It required a five-week stay in Lismore although this time around it wasn't as bad, I could drive to Brisbane or alternatively the family could visit me in Lismore if need be.

I found the rehearsal process for this play a bit strange. I felt that not enough time was actually spent on rehearsing the play. It came as no surprise to me when the date for the opening crept up on us and the play was incomplete. Initially, I looked at it as five weeks wasted, but then realised you take away the experience and accumulated knowledge and apply it next time around. The play itself was an outdoor performance and moved throughout Lismore, ending with a scene being staged on the back of a big truck by the river. It appeared that the whole community had gotten involved. I found the whole outdoor experience interesting, not to mention getting to know and work with some interesting characters among the actors. One of them, Neville, offered advice on a play I had written earlier that year titled *Blak Velvet*, which is yet to hit the stage.

'Aim for forty pages at least. As long as you've got that you've got enough material to play with.'

There was also a female that I'd met in Lismore who said something to me that I have never to this day forgotten. We were yarning and sharing each other's experiences one day, talking about work when I mentioned my poetry.

'So you're a poet?'

'Well, I write what looks or sounds like poetry I suppose.'

'Darling, you sound like you've had somewhat a sheltered life. You need to have your heart ripped to shreds before you can understand passion, anger, love and pain. Only then will you be able to write with full understanding.'

I just looked at her; I did not know how to respond. My silence prompted her to continue.

'You've been with the one guy all your adult life, he waits on your every beck and call and has never cheated on you. You need to be hard done by, you need to experience being taken for a ride, or be used and then spat out and rejected.'

Oh my God, I thought to myself. I don't think I want to experience any of that just so that I could qualify to write poetry, or worse still, write at all. I loved my life. I loved my family. I loved being married to Danny regardless of all his little idiosyncrasies. Which, to be honest, drove me nuts – his dry jokes or the way he ate his food really quickly as if someone was going to snatch it away from him, his burping or how long he spent in the toilet. To name a few.

Later that night I found myself wondering if my life really had been that sheltered. Was my heart too loved and protected? I thought back to how quickly Dan and I got together. There'd been no competition. He had left his previous girlfriend quite easily for me, been loyal to me the whole time and treated me like I was the only woman on earth. He made me feel so special, like I could do or say anything and he would always love me and be there for me, no matter what. He had this way of looking at me that made me feel I didn't even have to try with him, because he just desired me. Was all this stunting my growth as an artist or writer? Should my life be disrupted in order for me to grow? I almost began to resent what Dan and I had. Maybe I wasn't being challenged as a person.

While in Lismore I received a phone call from the Arts Council about auditions for a play titled *Yesterday Now* written by Indigenous playwright Anthony Newcastle. Immediately I indicated my interest and it was decided that the director along with Anthony and the other actor would travel to Lismore rather than me travel to Brisbane.

On the day of the audition I couldn't wait for the trio to arrive. The director turned up.

'How ya going, Steve Gration.' He immediately extended his hand.

We soon learnt that the other two were caught up somewhere and would be another hour or so before they arrived. The director decided to go ahead with the audition without them, which I was happy about as I wasn't sure I wanted all three of them present anyway. Afterward, Steve decided to stay and watch rehearsals until the other two arrived.

Mid-rehearsal the other two joined Steve way up the back. I was both excited and nervous knowing that a small audience was watching and that they'd be checking me out. Afterwards, I joined them.

'Hi, I'm Anthony.' I shook the hand of this strikingly tall, handsome blackfella whose voice resembled soothing, distant thunder.

'Oh and this young fella over here is Tom.'

Tom extended his hand. He had a humbling, sincere energy about him that was comforting.

'Pleased to meet you, Tom. Shall we go and get some lunch somewhere?' I asked.

We walked to a kebab shop just around the corner. As Anthony, Steve and I talked, Tom sat by the door, seemingly preoccupied. When it came time for me to return to rehearsal, I bid the three of them farewell.

'Let me know whether I got the part or not soon,' I said to Anthony. 'I'm real busy but would like to make time for your play if you guys want me.'

And with that I was off. I had no idea how I must've come across to them.

After wrapping up *The Flood*, I started rehearsals with Tom and Steve at the Queensland Arts Council building at Dutton Park. Before we knew it, Tom and I were on the road for our metropolitan area tour. I did not know what hit me, having forgotten how intimate working in this area could become. I had experienced close contact during my training days at Naisda, but now my only close contact was with my husband and my daughters. I had lost sight of what it was like to touch another person, stare into their eyes or make funny faces and sounds without cracking up. I had given myself permission to go to these places with Tom during rehearsals, but the biggest shock was once we hit the road together we had to occupy twin-share rooms for overnight stays. I hardly knew this whitefella and felt really uncomfortable, but I decided not to make a big deal for fear of being considered a prude. I told myself it was cool and, besides, it allowed us both to save our dollars.

One time, though, I couldn't sleep. Tom was out to it. I lay there listening to him breathing. At home during times like this I would usually roll over and indicate to Dan to entertain me and of course he would oblige. I could just see the outline of Tom's body. Inappropriate thoughts made their way into my head.

> *I am entangled with this whitefella as if snakes interlocked. I am aware that where we are is sacred ground, high up on the top of a mountain. We lay on a bed of white feathers. Feathers are everywhere and also stick to both our completely naked bodies. I can hear giggling around us, but cannot see anyone. It is my sisters spying on the business we are engaged in.*

I woke up covered in sweat with my thighs squeezed tightly together. Thank God it was only a dream.

A couple of days later Dan and I were sharing some quiet time in the lounge.

'Dan?'

'Yeah.'

I told him about the dream.

'Do you think it means something?'

'What do you mean?'

'Well, do you think it's a warning?'

'Don't be silly, woman,' he snapped. I could tell I'd hit a nerve.

'You'll be fine once you finish this tour. Youse are just spending a lot of time together, that's all.'

I really needed to hear that.

We had a couple of days break before continuing on with the tour. Tom had driven from Southport on the Gold Coast, and was tooting the horn loudly in the driveway. It was raining and cold. The heater in the lounge enticed me to stay indoors and continue sleeping, but the importance of making money sprang to mind. I peeped through the curtains straight into Tom's eyes. My belly kicked as the memory of the dream surfaced. I smiled and waved indicating I'd be there in a tick. Tom waved back.

'I'm off,' I whispered to Dan, as I kissed him gently. 'Kiss the girls for me. See you hon.'

I brave the cold and head toward the car.

'Morning,' Tom said as I settled myself in.

He knew I wasn't good in the mornings, not at the best of times. It usually takes me a while to start functioning.

I smiled back as he reversed onto the street.

By the end of our tour, around the middle of 2004, I had been broken-in in terms of touring etiquette, if there is such a thing. I'd given myself permission to let go of my set ways and Tom and I did everything together, from eating to travelling to sharing the same room. I had made a transition from wife and mother to independent woman and allowed myself to get close to my co-actor. Probably too close. When our touring came to an end I experienced withdrawals.

The following week I was on the phone to Tom.

'What's wrong with me? I miss touring and performing and the whole package that comes with it.'

'That's normal, Fi,' he reassured me. 'Everyone goes through it.'

'Yeah, but I'm not everyone, I should be happy that I'm back home with my family.'

'It'll pass, don't worry, trust me.'

I focused on re-establishing a routine with the family, especially with Justice and Ebony as Sheridan was going through the 'I don't want to know my mum' stage by then.

CHAPTER TWENTY-ONE

Following the *Yesterday Now* tour I was simultaneously offered two more touring jobs. One was to return to Vancouver to participate in the Talking Stick Festival; the other to tour several states back here in Australia with Real TV. After much thought I decided to remain in the country with Real TV and work with the cast and crew of *Children of the Black Skirt*, a play written by Angela Betzien. The play was the school version of *The Orphanage Project* that I had done back in 2003 with QTC. I had worked with these guys before, so felt pretty comfortable with taking this job on, although it would mean leaving the kids behind.

Up until that point Dan really hadn't had much luck finding decent employment. He'd got some work with BoysTown as a youth worker, but the position did not last. I was fast becoming frustrated with the fact that in order for us to make some kind of income I had to keep leaving the girls. But I loved performing again, and I really saw this work as a second chance – I considered it a privilege and was sincerely grateful. Still, I wanted to choose when to tour and when to stay at home. I took my growing resentment to Dan one day.

'Danny, when you gonna get a job? I don't like leaving the girls all the time. Please just get a job, anything.'

'Be patient, woman. No-one said it was gonna be easy. It'll work out.'

I remembered Danny telling me back in Weipa that he would have no problem finding work once we moved to Brisbane, but kept my mouth shut. The conversation was uncomfortable enough as it was.

'But why is it so difficult? Surely there are Murri organisations that can help.'

'Fiona, give it a rest will ya,' Danny snapped.

I backed off and decided to focus on the *Children of the Black Skirt* tour ahead of me. I had a week or so to learn the play before we were scheduled to fly to South Australia for two weeks.

The content in the play was a very important part of Australia's history and I thought that Angela Betzien had done well attempting to portray the Indigenous aspect considering she was non-Indigenous. The play was a gothic fairytale for young people and was told through the eyes of three lost children who discover an abandoned orphanage in the bush. They learn a history of Australia – from convict times to World War II to the stolen generation and beyond – through the spirits of children who once lived there. If any part of the character or dialogue seemed inappropriate or incorrect to me I felt obliged to voice my concern. Both the director and Angela were great about this, very respectful; they were so passionate about their work and sensitive to black–white issues affecting this country. We did not always agree with each other, but on the whole we worked with mutual respect, professionalism and friendship.

Adelaide was great. It was the first time I had been to the city and I loved being there. There was, however, a difficult situation with the stage manager. She had been great for the majority of the tour, but over time I noticed that whenever she was directing an order to me she had a somewhat condescending way of speaking, which was not the case whenever she was talking to the other two actors. It was as if she was annoyed with me or impatient about something. I held back, taking into consideration that stage managers are a rare breed and like things done a certain way. After one performance, though, the three of us actors started packing the set, as we usually did, when the stage manager joined us. By now I had learnt that it was a rule to take the set and place it straight in the back of the vehicle as opposed to 'double loading'. The other two actors were double loading, but the stage manager was not saying anything. She was in the back of the van giving instructions when I approached with a load. She snapped at me about the technique I was using, accusing me of making unnecessary work and wasting time. I was shocked. A directive was one thing, but negative superiority was another. However, I didn't say anything. Instead I thought, no, we're all tired, she's obviously tired, just leave it. No sooner were we all in the van and set for departure than once more she had a shot at me. Right, I thought, this woman wanna go. Before I knew it I became verbally aggressive, informing her that if she kept it up she wasn't going to get any cooperation from me. Who the hell did she think she was thinking that I was gonna respond with a 'yes miss, no miss, anything you say miss'? It was quite apparent that this wannabe bigshot had assumed she had acquired her own little Jacky Jacky that she could play boss woman to. For her own good she backed off once I made it quite clear that I wasn't going to pardon her approach any longer.

Apart from that business and a couple of other little tiffs us girls had, I loved the whole experience. As the tour progressed, I began to notice that almost everywhere we were booked into there were spirits present, mainly of young white females from early childhood through to mid-twenties. Their energy was never angry or scary, quite the opposite in fact. Sometimes they seemed to want to tell me something. Often the younger spirits appeared sad as well. They would hang their heads low and I'd sense their heavy hearts, but that would be as far as these encounters would go. It got to the point where the other girls were not prepared to share a room with me for fear of getting caught up in my many encounters.

The most full-on incident was at Victor Harbor, down the bottom of the South Australian coast. It was only an overnight stay as we were off to Kangaroo Island in the morning. Around midnight I woke up to the sound of an old steam train pulling up and tooting loudly. My door opened and just outside my room I could see people getting on and off the train in a rush. They appeared to be dressed in attire from the twenties and thirties. A bright, beaming light shone on me, causing me to sit up and squint at them, slightly annoyed at all the commotion. What is wrong with these people? Aren't they concerned at all about the noise they're making? And at this hour? Next thing an old white man dressed in a red, blue and white uniform appeared at my door. He appeared to be in a huge hurry and somewhat annoyed at my presence. In his hand he carried a bucket and on his head he wore a conductor's hat. He was very old with a long, gaunt face. He walked up to me, then proceeded to circle the bed, keeping his eyes on me the whole time. Next minute he was floating, looking directly down at me. And then – just like that – he exited the room, slamming the door behind him. I heard the train toot and pull out, leaving me in complete darkness and silence. I turned the bedside light on and kept it on until morning. I couldn't wait to ask the other girls if they had been woken up by the noise, as well.

The following morning we all gathered out the back, packed and ready to go with a few minutes to spare.

'Hey, did you girls hear that train last night?'

One of them shot me a confused look.

'Fi, what are you talking about?'

'Uhm, the train that came about midnight.'

Laurel and Jody looked at each other. Jody seemed more concerned than Laurel, who had always been in her own world.

'Fi, aah, no train comes past here.'

'Excuse me, you two, but I was woken up by it. And the rudest old whitefella came into the room and was looking at me like I had no right to be there or something. Seriously, my door opened, I heard the tooting and everything. Surely youse musta heard it. Look there's even train tracks.' I pointed at them.

'Yes, but look at where they end, Fi,' exclaimed Jody.

What the hell? Sure enough, the tracks ended about twenty metres to the right, just past where we were parked. I felt like a complete fruitloop. It's a wonder they didn't put me on the plane there and then and send me off to a psych ward.

I spotted the hotel gardener pottering around and made my way over to him.

'Excuse me, sir, but does a train pull in here . . . at all . . . at any point . . . for some reason?'

He kept on with whatever he was doing and then, without looking at me, responded.

'You heard the train as well.'

I knew it, I knew I wasn't wonky upstairs, well not *that* wonky anyway.

'Several people have claimed to hear the ghost train from time to time.'

'Excuse me, did you say ghost train?'

'Yep, that's exactly what I said. No train pulls up here. Well, not for a long time.'

He went back to busying himself among the shrubs. I headed back to the bus and climbed on quietly.

Arriving on Kangaroo Island later that day was exactly what we all needed. The place was absolutely beautiful. We were given a gorgeous beach house that overlooked the open sea and mud flats. Driving from one end of the island to the other I could feel spirits of old people everywhere.

'Uhm, Fi we're not particularly interested in sharing a room with you. Your little encounters are kinda weird,' said one of the girls as we walked through the house inspecting it.

I sort of just laughed it off. I didn't really want to be alone, but made out that it was nothing. Nothing happened that weekend, though. I had the most peaceful night's sleep. Our South

Australian tour was almost wrapped up. I couldn't wait to see Dan and the girls.

My ongoing association with QTC worked to my advantage all-round. Not only was I getting regular work and gaining experience and exposure, but I was also getting paid to make up to two visits a year back home delivering movement and drama workshops with the cast and crew from Real TV. These trips required us girls to work with the children from the Western Cape campus, both primary and secondary, as well as the Napranum campus. I continued to deliver dance movement classes, as well. In between workshops we performed *Children of the Black Skirt* to the communities. I absolutely loved it. I got to see the family on a regular basis, especially Nan, who was becoming more and more withdrawn. She rarely spoke, but was still active. She would regularly walk from Lyn's place over to her old place at 1 Peppan Street and back, stopping on the way to check the mango, custard apple, lemon and guava trees she had planted back in the eighties for fruit. Then she'd pick the rake up and proceed to tackle the never-ending flow of mango leaves. It didn't matter that the leaves just kept falling.

It was a pleasure for me to open up my family to my co-actors and, in turn, my family embraced them. The girls got on really well with my nieces and nephews and before you knew it Leti, Jody and Laurel knew most of the rude words in Alngith and Napranum home language.

'Say *moorasee*,' instructed Brittany, articulating slowly.

'*Moooraaaseeee*,' said Laurel very slowly, bursting into laughter.

Leti laughed so hard she almost keeled over. All my nieces and cousins laughed as well.

'*Chay* you now, Leti, you say it. You can also say *ngooraaseee*.'

'Teach me another word then. Actually what does *moorasee* mean?' she queried.

'*Moorasee* is *moorasee*,' sang the girls.

'Give the English word, silly,' chipped in Kathleen.

'*Mooоraaseee* is snot.' They all laughed again.

'Okay Leti and Laurel, come closer now, we gonna teach you rude words.' The girls huddled in closer. I knew exactly what words were being exchanged. The biggest laughter erupted among them, which continued on all the way to the beach, as the two white girls from the city practised their Napranum slang and dialect.

Apart from performing in town and working with the schools, the highlight for me was performing in the undercover area of my old primary school at Jessica Point. This was where I had experienced my first dance class and realised that the performing arts was something I wanted to be a part of. To be back there, contracted by the state's leading theatre company to share my skills with my people, both young and old, gave me a real boost.

CHAPTER TWENTY-TWO

At some point during 2005 our landlord had decided to sell. We did not want the children to have to leave their school, so decided to remain in Capalaba. I hated the fact that we hadn't bought a house by that stage. I kept holding my breath and hoping that Danny would get a job and all would be back to normal. My resentment about Danny's lack of success with stable, decent employment continued to slowly grow. Regardless, I kept telling myself that everything would be alright in the long run, that it was just a phase we were going through and that eventually we would stabilise. Of course we would; we wanted nothing but the best for the girls, for us as a family, and Danny and I would do whatever it took.

I'm lying on our bed in our room facing toward the mirror. No-one else is at home, it's just me. Thoughts of our future are preoccupying my mind space. I'm concerned for our future financially. I strongly feel that things are only going to continue to get worse. By that stage it appears that the chance of Danny getting work is really slim. I really don't know what's going to happen to us. I begin to doubt Danny's ability to provide for our family.

A heavy, dark feeling enters me through the tip of my head and slowly seeps its way down through my body, filling every cavity and fabric throughout. It's fear like I've never known before. It's dark and heavy and strong. I know and know deep in my belly that something bad awaits us as a family.

I told myself that the move was only temporary and that we'd be fine in the long run. At least the girls still had the friends they had made since our arrival early the previous year. This house was much smaller, but I kept reassuring myself that as long as the girls were safe, fed, warm, loved and healthy I really didn't have anything to complain about. There were always others in worse situations – always. Besides, Dan now had something to work towards. We had received a gift of $10,000 from the trust fund representing my mother's tribal country to assist him in getting his own health-and-fitness business up and running. He had been working on the concept since graduating with a master trainer qualification from Australian Fitness Academy and intended to call his business Bora Fitness. He'd provide sessions in boxing, weight training and cardio fitness. He also began work as a fitness trainer at Aboriginal Centre for Performing Arts (ACPA) based in South Brisbane. Not long after that I joined him, briefly, as the course coordinator and then tutored contemporary Indigenous dance, as well as another couple of subjects.

Both of us absolutely loved working with the ACPA students regardless of the fact that we had quite serious concerns about the way things were done there. I was really focused on how I wanted to approach my role and how it related to the development of these Indigenous artists in training. A lot of talented, hungry students were coming through the doors and I felt that they needed a balanced approach to their cultural heritage and identity first in order to lay a strong foundation onto which they could build both professionally and creatively. If the position had been fixed and full-time I would've loved to have developed my role further, but the money I was making with ACPA just wasn't paying the bills.

To make ends meet, Dan also had a part-time position at a gym across the road where he taught aerobics classes using boxing training as his approach. I scored some more freelancing jobs in dance and choreography from time to time, which I was happy to take on, as by that stage I had decided to cut ties with QTC. So between the two of us crazily working around the clock the money started to come in again. It wasn't anything to scream about, but at least there was an income without me having to leave the girls behind.

I also contacted Tom about the possibility of him assisting me with my rewrite of *A Bastard's Tale*, which was scheduled for a Canada tour early in 2006. Fortunately, he jumped in the car and drove up from Inverell in New South Wales for a yarn. It had been about six or seven months since I had last seen him, so I was quite excited about getting together. I could see Tom jumping out of the car and immediately saying something funny. But here was someone who only resembled the Tom I knew back in 2004. He was half the size he had been. His face was gaunt and gone was the sparkle in his eye. Instead, a look that spelled pain remained.

I decided not to say anything, but just hugged him and after making a flippant comment about him 'losing so much weight' invited him inside. I had no idea what had happened, but decided to focus on the fact that he had made the effort to come all this way to discuss my play.

It's the middle of the night and Dan is right beside me with his hands over me. I'm on my right side facing toward the clothes cupboard. I suddenly feel my body go weak. I know what this means. A spirit is about to reveal itself to me. I open my eyes as I feel an extremely strong energy force right in front of me. I feel completely numb and unable to move. I try to wake Dan up by whispering his name, but am too weak to do so. The figure that appears floating in mid-air between our bed and the cupboard is that of a young white girl and appears to be about nine or ten years old. She has on a blue and white dress that is tied into a bow at the back, complete with stockings and style black shoes. She is very well dressed. She has blonde curly hair with a ribbon tying back the top section of her hair. As I look at her, she slowly lifts her right hand and points in an upward direction. She stays visible to me for probably no more than five seconds before disappearing. I whisper Dan's name once more and this time he hears me. He puts his arms around me and just holds me. His closeness soothes me and allows me to just relax in his arms. Her energy was so strong and so real it has left me shaking.

CHAPTER TWENTY-THREE

I knew it would only be a matter of time before fate and destiny had me planting my feet on Austrian soil. The invitation to accompany two Indigenous visual artists, Christian Thompson and Jenny Fraser, to Austria to present our works came out of nowhere and did not allow me much time to prepare. I knew I had to get on that plane. The rest would sort itself out.

Before I knew it my tickets were booked, accommodation sorted, incidentals paid, bags were packed and I was on my way to the airport via the Gateway Motorway bridge. The traffic was horrendous. I saw my check-in time come and go, and then my boarding time, and we still hadn't made it to the bridge. I bawled my eyes out.

'Get yourself together Fiona and call the airline,' instructed Danny, as he guided our car behind the long pile-up of congested traffic.

I dialled the number on the ticket and was surprised to hear a real person answer the phone. After explaining my situation between sobs I was even more surprised to hear the response. I was not to worry. The airline was aware of the congestion and many people booked to fly out that day had been affected. I was given my new flight number and time and encouraged to just ride the situation out with the assurance that I would definitely make my connecting flight out of Sydney.

'See woman, it always works out in the end,' came Danny's soothing voice.

While standing in line at Sydney waiting to board my Austrian Airlines flight the guy next to me struck up a conversation.

'First time to Austria?'

'Yes,' I nodded, smiling. 'You?'

'Nah. I'm originally from Salzburg but live here in Sydney. I make the trip back home once a year.'

He sounded as Aussie as.

'But you don't have an accent.'

'I guess that's a consequence of living here for the past twenty years.'

I thought of Dad. He'd been here since 1964, which put him over the three-decade mark, but his strong accent still remained.

'Where are you off to?' the guy asked.

'Vienna, Linz and hopefully Salzburg as well.'

His eyes lit up. 'Yeah? Why Salzburg?'

'My dad was born there but grew up in nearby Wals. I'm hoping I'll be able to visit my relatives.'

'Well, what d'ya know,' he replied with a smile on his face. 'I'll see ya when we get there then,' he replied, winking as we boarded.

I must've immediately fallen asleep as next thing I knew the pilot was saying we were about to cross the Australian border. At that point I felt both Mum's and Nan's spirits with me, acknowledging the track I was on at that point in my life.

Our stop at Kuala Lumpur could not have come soon enough although I got a huge surprise when I went to the toilet at the airport. Where exactly was the toilet seat? I realised the opening on the floor was it and I'd have to squat over it. My God, I thought to myself, I'd wanna aim right otherwise big shame job. Why would anyone want to make going to the toilet this challenging? I wondered what other culture shocks awaited me once I got to Austria.

Hours later I was woken up by the smell of breakfast. It was only a few hours before we'd be landing. A couple of hours from Vienna I lifted the window shutter to a smoky, foggy sight outside. I placed my head against the window and just took in the sights. I could feel and see Dad's smiling face as we commenced our descent. As the fog cleared away a land of rolling hills and green meadows revealed itself.

The first thing I noticed about Austrians was that they rarely smiled. They seemed stressed out permanently and had harsh faces. As I made my way through customs, the lady who stamped my passport had a ciggy dangling from the corner of her mouth and she seemed more annoyed than anything else. There was no warm smile or 'Welcome to Austria' greeting, nothing.

Just stamp, then next and so on, very militant. In the main section of the airport I looked for the word Vienna. It was nowhere to be seen, although the word Wien was everywhere. I thought of Dad warning me that I should make an effort and learn 'at least a little bit of German to get you through'.

I needed to contact my cousin Ulrike and let her know that I had arrived. When I emailed her to say I was coming to Austria she had insisted I call her. Ulrike, her husband and their two kids lived in Vienna while the rest of the family were in Wals. I needed some coins to make the call so I strutted up to the shop and asked for 'five dollars worth of coins please'.

The shop attendant gave me a weird, annoyed look and proceeded to serve the person behind me.

'How rude,' I thought to myself, but then I realised that I needed euros. I decided to buy a packet of cashews and use the change to call Ulrike.

The connecting flight to Linz was really quick, only about thirty to forty minutes. I was so excited to see the other artist Jenny Fraser waiting at the airport for me. Yay! I thought to myself. Someone I can talk to.

Past the airport security who were dressed in black and armed with guns I quickly trotted aiming straight for Jenny. After checking in at the Ibis, which was straight across from the Linz train station, I hit the bed. Once we were all rested and settled Jenny suggested we meet for dinner and acquaint ourselves with each other and the program details. It turned out that I had several days free before our hosts were scheduled to pick us up and take us onto Kollmitzburg where we would stay for about a week before heading onto the art station for our individual presentations.

I soon got a phone call from Ulrike. The family were all driving from Wals and would come to the hotel. I couldn't believe it. I was about to meet my Austrian relatives for the first time.

As the time drew near my emotions were all over the place. I went out onto the balcony of my hotel room. A couple of seconds later I could see four adults, an older male and female and two younger females, get into the lift. I knew it was them. As they walked toward me I immediately felt familiar spirits and blood, particularly when I looked into my dad's brother's eyes. My uncle hugged me long. He pushed me back, looked directly at me again and then hugged me once more. My aunty appeared strong and wise, she had a serious look on her face, but her eyes were soft. Andrea seemed stand-offish, but I did not buy into it. Ulrike and Andrea mainly did the talking as their parents had very little English. The flow of conversation was slow, but I did not feel uncomfortable at all.

'We are driving to Wals, yeah?' asked Andrea.

'Now?' I enquired.

The parents smiled and nodded.

'Okay,' I shrugged.

I proceeded to gather some things into a bag even though I had no idea where Wals was or how long it would take. I was with my family in the middle of Europe; I really didn't care where we were going. Before we set off we hugged Ulrike goodbye. She'd hook up with us again later.

I loved the drive to Wals. Andrea kept me busy in conversation the whole way, briefly speaking of Austria's political and economic situation and mentioning their gaining independence after signing a treaty in the mid fifties.

'We have made considerable progress as an independent county and we are doing quite well economically. Our standard of living is quite high now.' She appeared to be very proud of her country and wanted to share this with me.

'So, Andrea, where do you live? Do you live with aunty and uncle?'

'No, I live on my own. We will drive past my unit, I will show you.'

'Okay,' I smiled.

'You are also to meet Clause.'

I remember him from the photos Dad had shown me over the years. He is my other cousin and the only son of my uncle.

My uncle turned onto a winding little dirt track.

'Up ahead is the farmhouse where Uncle Fred grew up along with my father,' Andrea explained.

Then something bizarre happened to me. All of a sudden I couldn't see. Everything had gone completely black. I just sat there and let whatever it was run its course. As suddenly as it appeared it went away, allowing me to catch sight of the old farmhouse as we approached it.

My uncle drove very slowly, allowing me to have a good look. I could almost see my Austrian granny peering back at me from inside. It was as if heaven had just opened a door especially for me and ordered it to run a river of blessings over me. We made our way to my uncle's place opposite the old farmhouse. Obviously he, too, had a knack for gardening. The walkway that led up to his front door was lined with flowers and shrubbery in many colours. Sweet plums dangled from trees no taller than me, like guards protecting my uncle's handiwork. Flowers dangling from window boxes waved greetings of welcome. An oleander had been planted just outside the front door.

'Oleander,' said Andrea as she pointed to it.

'I know. I love the smell of oleander, it reminds me of death and funerals.'

She gave me an odd look, but proceeded to direct me inside. I didn't have time to explain exactly what I meant by that, I was overtaken by what was unfolding before me. Oleanders, frangipanis and the bleeding heart were flowers that were always readily available to pick for funerals around the community during my childhood. The mere scent of them always brought back these memories, even years later.

My aunty and cousin led me upstairs to my room.

'This was Ulrike's room,' Andrea pointed out. 'Take your time to settle in.'

As she pulled the door behind them, my aunty smiled at me comfortingly. I smiled back. I immediately felt several spirits in the room, but Dad's presence was the strongest. He was smiling at me constantly and I could sense a real proud look on his face. I sat facing the window and looked across to the farmhouse. I couldn't believe it. Here I was in Wals with the house Dad grew up in right in front of me. It was like a picture out of an old European storybook. The farmhouse was huge and old. I could imagine Dad living there as a child. In my mind I could see my grandmother, a young woman doing it alone with two young sons to care for. The wind had blown me all the way across the globe so that I could place my eyes on my father's land, his home, his history. My childhood prayers had been answered. I sat there and wondered what exactly it was that I had done to deserve such experiences. I wanted to get closer, so I made my way downstairs.

'Can I go across the road and look at the old house?'

Andrea assured me it was fine.

'There are people renting the house though, so just maybe walk around the outside.'

'Okay,' I agreed, although I would've much preferred to go inside.

The house seemed to greet me as I walked toward it. I sensed the spirit of my granny on me. I proceeded to the left of the house and slowly circled it, running my hand along the outside. When I reached the back I peered in through the window. I really couldn't see anything, but could tell it was the kitchen. I so wished I could go inside. My father played here as a child, and now here I was walking the same ground. Once I'd breathed in enough I made my way back across the road.

My uncle suggested I accompany him to his vegetable garden and what he did once we got there spun me out. He went straight for the strawberry patches, found the biggest, ripest strawberry, snapped it, dusted it off and handed it to me to eat. Oh my God! This is exactly what Dad did when I first visited him at Gosford. What does it mean?

We all decide to drive into Salzburg for a look around and lunch. I was blown away by the churches, museums and by how massive the buildings were. During lunch my uncle and I got into a bit of a debate about of the plight of the Jews versus the Australian Aboriginal people. With Andrea as our translator, I realised I was locking horns with my uncle in much the same way I did with Dad. Andrea sensed I was getting upset.

'Don't worry about him, he's stubborn and opinionated.'

'So am I,' I responded. 'But I don't want to waste time arguing.'

'Then don't,' she instructed me. 'Just let it be.'

I nodded at my wise, stern cousin, and decided I would let it go, as frustrating as that was for me to agree to disagree.

After lunch we hit the streets to do some shopping and sightseeing. The next stop was visiting my granny's grave site. I immediately cleaned the cobwebs away and pulled up the weeds that had taken up residency. I was then instructed to light a candle to signify my presence. I knew this woman; she was the silent, absent granny in my life, my blood. I kneeled beside the headstone, placed my hand on it and read the wording.

Anna Wirrer
Geb. Wallman
***25. Marz 1909 in Vigaun**
17. November 1993

With a start I realised she was still alive when Sheridan was born. If only I had started my search earlier.

Later that day we went to the pub where Dad apparently had his first drink. I was led through the old bar and out the back where huge mountains served as a backdrop. As I sat facing them I heard someone storming their way through the pub.

'Where is my Australian cousin? Where is she?'

I turned around just in time to see this more than six-feet-tall man stomping his way toward me. Before I could prepare myself, he scooped me up and started kissing me. My feet dangled helplessly in midair before he plonked me back down.

'Finally, we get to meet you. I am your cousin, Clause.'

'Hi Clause, how ya going?'

He let out the biggest laugh.

When a couple of waitresses come to take our order they looked at me, then back to my uncle, smiling the whole time. They pointed to their faces. It was clear that they were discussing my nose and cheekbones. Then they rubbed their arms and I heard the words 'Australian Aborigine' followed by nods of acknowledgement.

When our meals arrived I realised everyone else's was quite large compared to my pumpkin soup. No-one said anything, but later that evening it all made sense. I was somewhat starving by this stage and couldn't wait to devour dinner. You can imagine my surprise when they served up a bowl of soup made out of mushrooms that Clause and his young son had picked especially for me from the mountains, accompanied by a traditional type of dumpling known as *Knödel*. Andrea must've read my mind.

'That is why we ordered such a large serving at lunchtime. The middle of the day is when we have our main meal and in the evening we have something light.'

'Oh, now you tell me.'

Now I don't like mushrooms at all, but whatever it was my aunty put inside that soup and dumpling I could not get enough of it.

The following morning I was sitting with my aunty and uncle having breakfast. They were speaking in German while I replied in English – they would point to a kettle, so I would hold up my cup. I recognised the room we were in from when Dad had first shown me photos of them back in 1996. Now here I was at the same table. After Andrea joined us they asked me about my relationship with Dad's wife. I was honest and upfront with them.

'Not good,' I told them. 'I don't think she likes me. I don't think she accepts me.'

Andrea relayed that my uncle wanted to know if Dad had left me anything.

'Photos, an old dictionary, information about our ancestry and Granny's cloth that she stitched in 1924,' I told them.

'Anything else, has he left you anything else?' Andrea continued.

'Like what?'

My uncle started to speak once more.

'Dad says that a parent must leave an inheritance for his children. You and the girls should have received something, surely.'

I shook my head and explained that there had been no will made known to me even though Dad had mentioned it on several occasions. I decided then and there to tell them everything that happened leading up to and following Dad's death. I informed them that when I made enquiries about Dad's will, I was told the girls and I had been left nothing, even though although we were his only living blood relatives. I explained that this didn't make sense to me considering the conversations I'd had with Dad. He would not have lied to me, nor would he have changed his mind. I smelled a rat. It seemed there had been some manipulation along the way, but I did not have the means to look into it. So, although my belly told me that something was not right, I had no choice but to just let it go.

My uncle became quiet and looked sad, but my aunty was coming across as mad. She started to clear the table and do the washing up.

'Andrea, what is she saying?'

'Mum doesn't like your father's wife. In her opinion she says she is not a good person and did not deserve Uncle Fred.'

Everyone reaps what they sow. There are consequences for every action in due course. That night I fell asleep with such thoughts swimming around in my mind.

The following day the plan was to take me up the same mountain that Dad had told me about – the one that overlooks Wals.

'When you go to Austria you must make an effort to go up it, Fiona,' he'd instructed, and here I was, about to do it with the family.

Clause and his family had accompanied us on this trip. He kept laughing at me as I freaked out more and more the higher we ascended toward the tip of Mount Geiereck (1806 metres) in the cable cart. The view from the top was absolutely breathtaking. Clause pointed out Wals to me as the clouds drifted toward us and through us.

I breathed in the moment.

They pointed out Germany to me.

'Oh, can we go there?' I asked.

'We probably won't have enough time but I'll see what I can do,' promised Andrea. They also pointed out Hitler's hide-out, basically cut into the side of a mountain. I noticed black birds around.

'They look like crows,' I said to Clause.

'These birds are known as *dohle* or alpine chough. Legend has it that when these birds cease to exist then so will Austria.'

'Wow!'

'You understand about such legends, yeah?'

'Of course I do. The crows are my maternal granny's totems. Our people believe the crow carries messages from families who have passed on. Nan would talk to the crow in her native dialect.'

Clause's face lit up. 'Would you like to feed the birds?'

I nodded, grabbing the bread he handed to me.

'Place your hand out.'

I did as told. The birds flew up to me, hovered in midair before eating off the palm of my hand.

Before we headed back to Linz, Andrea and I decided to go for a walk across the field near the house. She pointed to various places of significance and told me stories, but I sensed there was something on her mind. After a while she opened up.

'Fiona, why do you refer to yourself as bastard? Here in Austria it is not a good word.'

'It is what I've been referred to as by others since my childhood.'

'And it doesn't bother you?'

'Not really. Actually, it's what inspired me to search Dad out. I know I am so much more in worth than just a little word.'

CHAPTER TWENTY-FOUR

I reconnected with Jenny and Christian, my fellow artists, in time for our departure to Kollmitzburg. Fortunately for us, our hosts decided to pick us up and personally drive us there although the original plan had been for us to catch the train. As I sat quietly in the back of the van listening to the conversation flow I took in the sights. I realised the others had all met before and that both Jenny and Christian were already known in Austria for their works. Christian, who is of the Bidjara nation, was presenting his *Emotional Striptease* series as well as screening a video work titled *The Fox* that explored introduced species in Australia. Jenny, an artist and curator from Yugembah/Mununjali, screened *A Dark Day at Sea* and exhibited a series of works titled *Hit the Road* that examined Australian road-kill. Mid-conversation the wife turned to me.

'So, Fiona, what exactly is it that you do?'

Before I could answer Jenny stepped in and told her about my writing and performing and then proceeded to explain my connection with Austria and the one-woman play I had written as a result of discovering that side of my heritage.

The host smiled.

'I look forward to your presentation very much, Fiona.'

I absolutely loved where we stayed for the most part of the week in preparation for our presentations at the art station, which was about a thirty-minute drive away. It was a two storey house, right beside the Danube, the longest river in the European Union and Europe's second longest after the Volga. The majority of our time consisted of short walks, writing, visiting the little village across the river and quiet time. Unfortunately, I got into some disagreements with our host.

'You must eat and not waste,' he ordered after noticing the food left behind on my plate. 'Eat, eat, eat!'

'I can't if I'm full,' I told him. 'That would not make sense.'

'Ahh, but it is such a waste, is it not?'

'Don't make so much food then. Let us prepare our own. That way we make only what we need and will be able to eat it all up.'

He picked up the tray and headed back to the kitchen.

'Thank you, though,' I called out.

He looked back at me.

'For breakfast. Thank you. I appreciate it.'

He nodded and he continued on.

The time for us to present our respective works arrived. We were to stay at the art station for the remainder of the trip, so had to pack and relocate. I chose the room right at the top of the art station where the sky could be seen through a transparent ceiling. Staring at the stars as I drifted off to sleep was awesome. Wandering through the gallery, which was just across from my room, I recognised artwork belonging to the Wik peoples and I realised our host must have had dealings with people from back home. I felt the old people's spirits around me. It was as if a little bit of home was with me in this faraway land. And imagine my surprise when we entered our host's workshop and there on the table was a large book opened at a page that displayed an artist from Aurukun. I spun out. Here I was in Austria and images of my people kept appearing.

The day came for us to present. I had been nervous initially until I realised I had a lot to share. I had copies of some of my books with me and had them for sale at the door. They all sold out. I also had a display of feather flowers, dilly bags, fruit mats, and the like. I presented some spoken word and played a recorded version of *A Bastard's Tale*. I spoke about my experiences and feelings surrounding my identity, and what it felt like to embrace both worlds. I paused for a second as I realised right in front of me were two of my cousins and my niece. My cousins had tears in their eyes. In fact, so did almost everyone in the audience.

When my cousins had first arrived that evening Andrea took me aside. She was carrying a plastic bag.

'Remember you said you were interested in placing your feet on German soil?' she asked.

I nodded, puzzled.

'Well,' she said, proceeding to tip the contents of the plastic bag onto the road, 'I brought a little bit of Germany to you. Now come here and place your feet on it and I'll take a picture, yeah?'

I smiled. I had always felt comfortable with Ulrike, but found Andrea to be more reserved. Yet here she was making an effort to do something weird, but special for me.

'You sausage, Andrea,' I said as I planted my feet in the soil and posed for a picture.

When Ulrike drove me back to Linz, Andrea came with us. We talked all the way. At one point Lena, Ulrike's daughter, began to cry in the back.

'What's the matter?' I asked Ulrike.

'She is frustrated that she cannot be part of the conversation. She wishes she knew English so she could speak with you.'

'Tell her I wish I could speak German. Maybe we should both learn each other's language so we can talk next time I visit.'

The remainder of my time was spent manoeuvring my way through the cobblestone streets of Linz in search of some souvenirs and gifts for the family. I spent time reading or daydreaming in the parks. I wandered through huge churches and marvelled at the infrastructure that towered above me. I couldn't get over how the Austrians appeared to love their buildings. The bigger and grander they were the better they were, it appeared. And it was nothing to drive past a castle.

Walking through the streets and markets wasn't always pleasant though. One day I was loudly yelled at by a cyclist as he sped past me.

'Yep, you enjoy your day too,' I called out as he flung his hands up in the air.

Another encounter was with a skinhead with the swastika sported on the sleeve of his jacket.

'Will you spare some change for the supreme race?' he

asked holding out his hands, as Jenny, Christian and I strolled by.

'Hey? If uncle the supreme race then what's he doing asking blackfellas for money?'

The three of us laughed, trying to make sense of his screwed-up attitude.

On the night before I was scheduled to fly out of Linz and on to Vienna, I had an interview with Austrian academic Agnes Neumeyer. It was good to have some company and I really appreciated the fruit and chocolate she brought as gifts, as I had nothing to eat in my room. We spent much of the allocated time talking about my biography of Nan.

'So would it be fair to say that *Whispers of This Wik Woman* is quite political?' she asked.

'Perhaps,' I said. 'I never really meant for it to be, though Nan, being who and what she was, inevitably created a political framework, I suppose. It's all part of life.'

'You are much like your granny, yeah?'

I shrugged. 'Maybe, I don't know. She's been the one constant in my life so far.'

When the interview was over Agnes gave me some gifts: the shell of a snail that had been handpainted to signify one of my mother's totems known in Mbaiwum as *tork*; a miniature bottle with the words 'Mozart chocolate liqueur' on the label, and a seven-centimetre root, symbolising my connection to Austria.

'You are a double native,' she said as she hugged me goodbye.

I gave her a confused look. Double native? I didn't quite know what to think of it.

'You belong to both Australia and Austria.'

CHAPTER TWENTY-FIVE

Not long after I got back both Dan and I, along with various other Indigenous dance artists from all over Australia, were invited to Canberra for a forum. Creating Pathways was supported by the Australia Council, the Aboriginal and Torres Strait Islander Arts Board, the Dance Board and Ausdance National and created a platform for topics such as industry learning, professional issues, maintaining networks, culture and professional SWOT analysis. Dan's sister, who lived at Victoria Point in Brisbane, looked after the girls therefore allowing both of us the chance to participate.

Some of the other dancers were people who we hadn't seen for eighteen to twenty years or so. What different pathways our lives and careers had taken since Naisda. Stephen Page was now leading Bangarra, the country's most successful Indigenous dance company. Marilyn Miller had been prominent in spearheading the direction and evolution of contemporary Indigenous dance. And

Gary Lang continued to plough new ground in dance in Darwin. Those of us who trained together during the late eighties and early nineties were now in our thirties and forties. Things were progressing in the industry and we could look back and track the immense progress made over the previous two decades or so. Opportunities to travel the globe were available whether you worked as part of a company or freelanced, as I now did. It was my work alone and not an association with a company that provided me with my profile.

Discussions held throughout the week were absolutely crucial to the development of contemporary Indigenous dance in this country, and were challenging to say the least. A key question that kept popping up was whether what we were doing was contemporary Indigenous dance or Indigenous contemporary dance? We never did reach a conclusion on that one. Maybe it was too early to be able to label this new creative ground.

I quickly realised how much I had missed singing and dancing. It had been absent from my creative expression for so long. But it was great to be reminded of the generation of dancers that we had once been a part of and recognise our respective development as twenty-first-century Indigenous artists since. To have the opportunity to yarn again with people such as Rita Pryce, Lewis Lampton and the rest was just deadly.

Late in 2005, I got a phone call from the principal of the Murri School in Acacia Ridge in Brisbane's south offering me a teaching position starting at the beginning of the new year. Did I keep freelancing and leaving my girls behind, or did I settle down and finally put that degree to use? It had now been several years since I graduated. After some thought I accepted the invitation on the proviso I could start after my upcoming Canada tour, which was to kick off in January. The principal agreed to this and said that Year 5 was mine on my return.

I could not see myself driving from Capalaba to Acacia Ridge every day, as I seriously hate driving, so we decided to move closer to the south. A bigger, four-bedroom house in Sunnybank was offered to us. It was just down the road from the secondary and primary schools, so we immediately packed up and moved. While packing I noticed that my wedding ring and the chain that Dad had bought me as a gift back in 1997 were missing. I turned everything inside out, but failed to find these two very significant pieces of jewellery.

We had no sooner set up the new place at Sunnybank than we were required to pack for Canada. Tom drove up to continue rewriting *A Bastard's Tale* in preparation for its performance in Vancouver. Marilyn Miller had helped us secure a space at Metro Arts on Edward Street in the city, allowing us to get stuck into it. It was different working with Tom this time around. He wasn't as happy or as enthusiastic about what we were doing as he'd been before. I almost felt like suggesting he forget about it and deal with whatever was consuming him, but figured that at least he'd made the effort and was here working with me. His energy was heavy and made me uneasy, but, regardless, we achieved what was important and soon the play was ready to go. A friend of Tom's offered to help and made the required sound recordings.

It was still good to be working with Tom again. I realised the little crush I had developed for him back in 2004 was gone – a gammon little crush, as a result of spending all that time together. I still got on well with him and even though he was obviously going through something really serious he was still making me laugh and feel good, which I wasn't getting from my husband. It was always worry, disagreements and serious talk those days with Dan.

Late one afternoon at the end of our rehearsal time Tom drove me home. It had been raining. I made a silly comment about how the rain affected me and we both laughed. I probably should not have revealed something so personal but this sort of talk was normal between us, even if slightly inappropriate. Tom found it amusing that I went into 'waiting to mate' mode both during showers as well as a storm. As he pulled up in front of the house he made a silly, flirty comment in return. I dismissed it, having noticed Danny draw back the curtain and peep outside.

'See ya,' I kissed and hugged Tom. 'Drive carefully and thanks for everything.'

I ran into the house and greeted my beautiful family. Later that night, though, the words that he said to me in the car played dangerously around in my head.

Early in 2006, Sheridan and Justice were put on the plane and sent up to the Cape to stay with Lyn while Dan, Ebony and I left for my Canada tour. A juvenile criminal record relating to a minor infringement when Danny was fourteen years old prevented him from travelling with Ebony and I through Los Angeles. He flew China Airlines through Taipei instead, which would have him arriving in Vancouver a day after our arrival.

Here I was once more tracking across the Pacific Ocean to share my works with our Canadian brothers and sisters, only this time I had my baby on the plane with me. Our descent into Auckland was nothing short of heart-stopping. The pilot informed us that conditions were stormy outside. I lifted the window shade up to be greeted with full-on rain and flashes of lightning all around. We had also begun to experience some turbulence. I noticed the air hostesses proceed to their seats and buckle up, as the plane continued to make its way through the storm. I looked around me. People were either gripping each other or the sides of their seats. Some had their eyes shut, praying I assumed, while others were just staring into space. A big drop jolted Ebony awake. She kept her little head on my lap and stared at me with her eyes wide open.

'Mummy, what's happening?' she whispered.

Another bump. She gripped me tighter around the waist.

'Nothing, bubba, it's just a little rainy and stormy outside that's all,' I reassured her.

'Why is the plane shaking?'

'Because *mboormbwin* is around. Don't worry, remember when *mboormbwin* dances it wants everything else to dance with it too?'

She nodded, but burrowed her head into my lap once more.

'Ebony?'

She looked up.

'Would you like to pray with me?'

She nodded and reached for my hand immediately.

'Lord Jesus, please put two angels at each of the wings of this plane and please may you yourself carry this plane down to landing. In your name we ask. Amen.'

'Amen,' I heard her whisper.

Immediately her little body relaxed as she slept on my lap until we landed.

Our stopover in Los Angeles was absolute chaos, the most challenging travel experience I'd ever had. I almost lost Ebony on the shuttle bus that transferred us from the airport to our plane. They had crammed so many people on the bus that Eb and I became separated. The lady who stood between us kept reassuring me that she could see Ebony and that it was cool. She introduced herself to me and told me that she was a Rockhampton girl and had grown up with a lot of Murris.

'Do you know the Doyles?' she asked as we shook hands.

'I'm married to a Doyle.'

Her eyes lit up as she shook her head. 'Oh my God, they're everywhere.'

On arrival at Vancouver Airport the immigration officials took Eb and I aside before directing us to a small room for further questioning. They had realised that Danny was unable to travel with us and was on a different flight. They needed to rule out the possibility of me having fled Australia with Ebony illegally, or that there was a custody issue.

Hours later we were finally able to leave and our host Margo Kane and her partner Bear greeted us. Margo, whom I had met during my first trip to Canada, is a beautiful woman and a performing artist from the Cree-Saulteaux nation and is known for her monodrama. She was the manager and artistic director of Full Circle First Nations Performance, which she had established in 1992. She established the Talking Stick Festival in 2001 with the aim of giving Aboriginal artists, both national and international, the opportunity to come together and share in a spirit of creative and artistic celebration. Bear, her partner, is equally as gorgeous. He is the tall, silent type. He sported a long ponytail and had a cruisy presence to match. I felt very comfortable with this pair and we yarned nonstop all the way to the hotel.

Early the next morning we woke up to Danny entering the room. Ebony was ecstatic and so was I. It was so good that two of my family members were here with me this time around. I didn't feel as alone as I did the last time and just wanted to get into it and give my best to everything.

Even though we were grateful for what we had been given, our room wasn't self-contained. I loved the view from our window, a magnificent sight of tall buildings, and the room was quite spacious, but Dan and I didn't want to eat takeout for the entire time we were there. Besides I wanted to be able to give Ebony breakfast at our convenience and cook whenever I could. When I mentioned this to Margo, almost immediately we were transferred across town to another hotel with self-catering facilities. This hotel was within walking distance to both my rehearsal space and performance venue, which was great.

My program for the two-week stay consisted of leading workshops in sharing cultural knowledge and giving presentations, as well as running information sessions on our work as Indigenous artists. My performance of *A Bastard's Tale* had been scheduled for the second week, at the Roundhouse Theatre. Tom had suggested that Ebony be written in to demonstrate trans-generational passing on of culture and so she would be hitting the stage with me. She was as excited, focused and confident as I would want her to be, a true little professional at six years of age. Tom's input really gave the piece more depth, I felt. He suggested that cultural props such as feather flowers and prepared ochre be incorporated, which provided much more symbolism. Sand was also used to depict my journey throughout time and country.

Danny was fitting in well. He loves meeting people and every chance he got he was off socialising. I didn't mind; I'm more of a hermit by nature and preferred only to leave the hotel for professional commitments. Besides, I found the cold weather almost paralysing, and Ebony wasn't enjoying it either. Mind you, I did make exceptions for shopping trips.

A young white Aussie girl attending university in Canada introduced herself to us. She was bubbly, wore a smile constantly and appeared proud to be a fellow Aussie. I loved this energy between us as Indigenous and non-Indigenous Australians connecting on international ground. I loved her display of affection toward us too and embraced the comradeship.

Halfway through our stay we were invited to go to the mountains and spend some time in a cabin. We were warned of the cougars and bears that inhabit the surrounding forest.

'Er, yeah, okay.' I looked across at Dan for his opinion.

'Why not? Ebony will love the whole snow experience.'

'Yeah, but I don't think I'll enjoy running from a cougar or a bear.'

Charles, who had invited us, laughed. 'Fiona, it will be fine, I promise.'

So Charles, Ruthie, a Full Circle employee, Dan, Ebony and I set off for the mountains. On our arrival, Charles appeared shocked as I got out of the car.

'Fiona, is that what you are planning to wear?'

'Why not? What's wrong with it?'

'In a couple of minutes you will not be able to feel your toes if you do not rug up this instant. Here.' He passed me a thick jacket and more appropriate shoes. 'And put these gloves on, the ones you have on are only suitable for city wearing. We are in the thick of it up here.'

I removed my gammon brown leather gloves and put on these serious-looking, thick gloves that immediately warmed my hands up. Soon we were trudging our way up the slippery slope in search of the cabin, which was several hundred metres away. The day was spent playing in the snow, building a snowman, snowball fighting and tobogganing. Ebony absolutely loved it and did not appear at all fazed by the cold. We ended the day with a meal inside the cabin before tracking our way back to the car. I don't think the Canada trip would've been complete if we had not have visited those mountains.

Toward the end of the trip I decided to give Ebony some pocket money and take her to Granville Island for some shopping. We caught the ferry over and I pointed out to her and Dan where I had stayed years earlier on my first trip.

A visit to downtown Vancouver opened up our eyes to the poverty that was prevalent in this city. Across the road a pregnant woman was prostituting herself and a beggar who had neither arms nor legs and was in a wheelchair approached us for money. Ebony asked if she could give him all her pocket money. She could not understand why he did not have a home and why he was so dirty and begging in the rain like that.

Following my performance one night we decided to walk back to the hotel rather than have Bear drive us back. Up ahead I could see a beggar. I felt Ebony squeeze my hand tighter as she too caught sight of him. We crossed at the lights and I noticed a ten-dollar bill on the pavement. I scooped it up immediately and put it in my pocket. As we got closer to the beggar Ebony tugged at me.

'Mummy, give that person the money you found. We don't need it. He does.'

I smiled at her. God had blessed me by putting such a beautiful girl with the warmest, most generous heart inside my belly to accompany me through life.

I stopped in front of the beggar, but he or she did not look up. I held out the money so they could take it.

'Thanks ma'am,' came the most awesome, deep voice from behind the covering that hid his face.

Just before I walked off he looked up. Hidden behind the covering I found myself peering into a pair of eyes that belonged to a strikingly handsome black man. He nodded at me in gratitude. I smiled at him and then joined Dan and Eb.

Wow, I thought to myself, what a presence! His face and voice remain with me to this day.

During Danny's presentation in the first week we had met a brother with Aboriginal ancestry who had been living in Vancouver for quite some time. Kevin seemed very excited about us being there and made no secret of it either. It was easy to see that his spirit needed to encounter home, people, blood, connection and history. He was hungry, and our presence appeared to be the very thing he needed to feed his sense of identity, which was clearly crying out for something, anything. He and his beautiful girlfriend invited us to their place for dinner. Kevin hunted for deer and Helen prepared the meal for us. Dessert included ice-cream topped with maple syrup that he had collected that afternoon from a maple tree especially for us. Ebony put so much of it on her ice-cream that she confessed to having a bit of a head spin. She thought it was the funniest thing that the syrup had made her 'drunk'. It was great to spend the evening with such beautiful, sincere people. As we left, they presented Dan and me with gifts symbolic of Helen's totemic lineage, and I understood it was a gesture not made lightly, not at all. I was absolutely honoured by the gift and acknowledged the spirit in which it was given to us.

CHAPTER TWENTY-SIX

On our return from Canada, Danny and I enrolled the girls at Sunnybank State Primary and Secondary. Both schools were just up the road from us, which was great. Not having to drive kids to school is half the job done, I reckon. I had also begun working at ACPA once more, so was juggling the two positions. On top of that I had continued to work on *Whispers of This Wik Woman*, with the aim of turning it into a stage play. Work on this had begun back in 2005 with Therese Collie with whom I was already familiar. Therese was the dramaturg with *A Bastard's Tale* back in 2002. Unfortunately, though, in 2006 Therese was unable to continue and another dramaturg had to be found and appointed. This turned out to be Janis Balodis who had written *The Flood*, the play that I had been a part of back in 2004. I found Janis tough to begin with, but after a while we found a place where we could collaboratively work and I learnt much under his guidance.

I was just beginning to settle into writing and performing again. I had a lot on my plate, but life was good. As long as I kept working we'd get there. The girls were making new friends. Well, not little Ebony, actually, she was experiencing bullying and name-calling in the classroom, but the older two appeared to be doing well. In short, they were all finding their respective grounds, in both schools.

I began teaching at the Murri School in February 2006. I was both excited and nervous. Excited because I couldn't wait to experience something new and implement all that theory that university had packed into me. Nervous because although I was a fairly confident person, performer and speaker, I had never actually been in charge of a classroom apart from prac teaching throughout my course. Another teacher had begun the year with my students before I started with them several weeks into the term.

From the second I walked into that classroom I asked myself, what the hell was this? And I'm not referring to the students or the school. I'm talking about the fact that you are responsible for someone else's child for up to six hours a day. You are responsible for their welfare, their learning, their behaviour, their wellbeing. There's a collective of these little people that you barely know and you are supposed to work and progress through not only their education but their overall wellbeing with them all. I found coordinating my own three daughters challenging enough and now here I was with thirty-odd students waiting for me to take them through their fifth year of primary school. I freaked out!

Regardless, slowly but surely I worked through every challenge, every unfamiliar encounter the best I could. I felt so inadequate in those first three months or so; I was an infant in teacher terms. I would take the silliest of questions to other teachers and fortunately for me everyone was so helpful and considerate. But the behaviour of the kids was the most challenging thing to contend with. One minute I had these beautiful children referring to me as aunty or even, at the slip of the tongue, as mum and next minute they'd be getting stuck into each other and causing the biggest disruption in the classroom. And the fighting, oh my goodness, they weren't just snickering at each other or sending a mean little look here and there – there were full-on punch-ups. Over and over again I had to keep reminding myself that the classroom wasn't the be-all and end-all of these children's existences. They had their backgrounds and home life experiences that I had to take into account and often I was up against those as well. I realised I couldn't just expect these ten-year-olds to be able to effectively leave other 'stuff' at the door. I had to make allowances, exercise flexibility, cater for individual learning needs, the list went on.

I also didn't anticipate how soon and how much the children and their issues and personalities would affect me. Before I knew it, I wanted to take some children home with me, look after them, untangle some of the behaviours that were clearly stunting their own growth and progress as well as that of their peers. I felt so much love and yet so much pain for these children; I saw them as my children, as me. These children were the future of my race, my people. My concern was where they were heading.

'Miss, can I come and stay with you please?' was a question too often asked.

'I'll see what I can do, bub,' would be my response.

I allowed too much into my heart and was on the verge of a collapse by around about the seven-month mark. I had been crying in the shower almost every night after work. It was not in relation to anything specific, more the whole challenge that came with the role. I felt like an ineffective loser and could not understand why I couldn't just get my act together and be like the other teachers. They all seemed to know what they were doing; they walked around looking all calm and cool. Why couldn't I just be like them? Was I really that incapable?

I'd stay up late preparing lessons and reading as much support material as I possibly could. I never took timeout for morning tea or lunch, but instead remained in my classroom making sure I had everything ready for the following sessions. I would stay back late as well, continuing to prepare even more. But after a while I somehow felt that I could not prepare enough. Quite simply I began to obsess.

I mentioned my concerns to Danny one day.

'Dan, I don't think I'm coping.'

'What do you mean?'

'I'm not enjoying work. I get anxious about going there. I don't feel relaxed and happy.'

'Fiona, give yourself a break. You've only ever known the arts business. This is your first year of teaching. You'll settle in and get the hang of it soon, give yourself some time to.'

Silence.

'Have you spoken to someone at school about how you're feeling?'

I was surprised that he had actually listened to what I was saying. Usually he would just dismiss the subject and tell me to get over it. I nodded.

'And what did they say?'

'Well same, they reckon it will get better over time.'

'There you go, everyone understands, just go with the flow.'

I did. I tried to ride the wave until one day I just knew something dramatic was going to go down. All it was going to take was one thing to push me over the line, I could feel something sitting there in my throat waiting for the chance to bust out.

I arrived at the door as I usually did, waited for the students to notice my presence and, hopefully, fingers crossed, they would and form into a straight line before I said good morning and opened the classroom. Phew! We were in the door. Now the next hurdle was getting them all to settle at their desks. Another five minutes, yep, now that's done, what's next on the agenda?

And on it went, step after step, systematically. The students had been working well in the mornings: roll mark, spelling test, times tables, diary writing. They were familiar with the routine. The chaos would arrive when those students who had completed their work had earned free time. Free time should be a good thing, but free time is also when talking and interaction happens, distraction occurs. How many times can you make someone sit in the corner, or send them to the principal's office, or expel them from an excursion? How many times can you go over the classroom rules, or how bright and obvious can they be posted up on the wall? I was getting over this business fast. As much as I loved the kids, I was, quite simply, running out of steam.

That day, the noise during free time had started to build, with bickering across the room slowly spreading.

'Stop swinging on the chair, Johnny.'

'Keep your voice down, Anthony.'

'No swearing, Dougie.'

'Keep your hands to yourself, Davinia.'

And on and on and on it goes.

Next thing I know a rubber comes flying through the air straight at me. I knew there and then that was it. That was where the *goona* was gonna stop flowing.

I grabbed my bag and walked out the door, straight up to the principal's office. I informed her I couldn't take any more, accused the kids of being unteachable, marched back down the stairs, and out the gate onto Beaudesert Road. I had so much steam to expel that I didn't notice how much distance I had covered on foot until Danny turned up and picked me up along the way.

Back at home I could not believe what I had done. What on earth had I been thinking? Although I wasn't really thinking at the time. I'd just gone with my emotions. I felt embarrassed and ashamed that I'd let everyone down – the students, the principal, the school and most of all myself.

Yet, regardless of this, I knew I did not want to return to that teaching situation anytime soon. About that I was adamant. I seriously doubted whether teaching was for me after all. I did not seem to have the required patience.

The principal was very understanding, upfront, considerate and fair. She asked me what I would prefer to do. I told her I was interested in trialling a dance program at the school. She agreed, and also gave me a week off to recover and prepare before returning to the school at the beginning of term four.

During 2006, an opportunity to travel to Sydney and Gosford, of all places, arose. It came at the right time. The spirits must've known I had to return to the Central Coast of New South Wales for some reason or another. The purpose of the trip was to promote my new publication *On Country: Stories of Nyrlotte*, a collection of stories from my childhood living in Cape country, roaming and exploring the land. I had written the majority of these stories back in Napranum and, after talks with UQP, I was given the opportunity to resurrect them. I had about seven already written and needed to write about three more to complete the manuscript. A contract was drawn up, and, as with *Whispers of This Wik Woman*, the editing and production phase took about a year before its publication in 2006.

Before meeting my commitments at the Sydney Writers' Festival – which consisted of panel discussions and presentations as well as networking with other Indigenous writers, one of them being Uncle Bob Randall – I went up to Gosford to give some talks and run workshops in the community and schools. Leonie Tyle, then children's publisher at UQP, accompanied me.

Someone who Leonie had been in contact with in the lead-up to our trip, a pleasant and respectful lover of literature, made himself known to me and offered to drive me around Gosford. During one of our drives around town I noticed a car that we had been trailing for several kilometres sported the words 'Austrian Spirit' on a bumper sticker. We also drove past the turn-off that

I swear was the road leading to Dad's property. The driver suggested we turn around and drive up to see if this was the case, but I declined his offer. I felt that I would not have been welcomed if his wife or any of her family had seen me. Instead I asked if I could be taken to Dad's memorial site. As we entered the crematorium all the memories of that day in 2002 came flooding back. I realised how much I missed having my father in my life. Why did he have to die? Why did he have to leave so soon after entering my life? This was so unfair. I could feel him close. I wanted to scream and yell at him for leaving so suddenly the way he did. I just wanted my dad back. I wanted to hear from him. There were so many questions still inside me. How could someone leave just like that? What the hell? Still, I knew that coming back here was a small step toward closure of all I had experienced during Dad's passing and funeral. It took a while to locate Dad's plaque, but, finally, we did. I was so grateful to have this quiet time with Dad. This trip wasn't really about my book at all; it was about this business.

Term four saw the beginning of a trial contemporary Indigenous dance program at the school, with students from prep through to Year 12 participating. Oh my God, what have I done? I went from the challenge of overseeing one class of thirty-odd students to roughly a hundred across the different grades. To begin with my sessions were compulsory for the students. It was difficult to introduce dance in a structured approach and environment, but we got through it and managed a performance at speech night where every single class presented a piece of choreography that they had learnt during the term.

Once more I was exhausted keeping up with the daily physical demands of stretch, demonstration, choreography, rehearsal and behaviour control, but this time I was enjoying it. I particularly loved sharing and exploring our culture through movement. My main focus was exploring the techniques, styles and movement expressions of both Aboriginal and Torres Strait Islander culture and building on those first and foremost. One of the main issues for me was the importance of adhering to cultural protocol wherever and whenever it was required. I was always mindful of imparting this knowledge to the students for their own personal growth in this very important aspect of our cultures.

Those students who were already familiar with traditional dance styles and forms got really excited when traditional movement forms were incorporated into more contemporary choreography. Their sense of cultural pride was clearly evident and it was a great opportunity for me. There were a few tensions though.

'Miss, my mum said us girls shouldn't be doing shake-a-leg, she wants to come and talk to you.' I was once told by a student.

'Why is that?' I asked.

'Because girls don't do shake-a-leg, only boys.'

'I can though,' I informed her.

'But you're a girl, miss, you shouldn't.'

'Nah, bub, where I'm from, we can. We just got different way of doing shake-a-leg to the boys, that's all.'

She gave me a confused look.

'If your mum still wants to talk just tell her to come see me and we can yarn about it, okay?'

She nodded and went to play with her friends.

Delivering those classes was a huge learning curve for me, as there was also the issue of differentiating between Aboriginal and Torres Strait Islander techniques, and then, on top of that, highlighting the differences between the various Aboriginal nations. I also had to be careful when it came to my own experimentation with dance. Growing up on Cape country and having exposure to Torres Strait Islander technique, it was inevitable that this would form part of my creative expression. The Torres Strait Islander students would ask me if I was in fact of Torres Strait Islander descent.

'No, I'm Aboriginal,' I would respond.

'But how come you know how to dance like us?' they would ask.

'Because I have been taught, or I, too, grew up with this type and style of dancing.'

I realised my movement vocabulary was obviously a fusion of the two nations.

I stayed at the Murri School for two more years, continuing in dance tuition and choreography. In addition, I was given the green light to create and deliver cultural studies units to complement what the kids were learning in dance. Attending the dance sessions had no longer been compulsory since the beginning of 2007; instead the students were required to audition for a place in the program. The rule of three strikes and you're out stood for the rest of the term, with students having to go through the whole audition process again if they wanted to get back in. This approach taught them the importance of focus, discipline, the responsibility of being held accountable for their actions, of fighting for what they wanted and being challenged to keep the privileged position of being a part of the dance troupe.

Over those two years I watched those students who loved to move and dance – whether it was hip hop, contemporary or traditional – continue to grow in terms of strength, commitment and respect. By the time we had weeded out those students who weren't serious, our classes had truly become productive and meaningful.

By 2008, I was working a four-day week teaching dance to Year 1 through to secondary, cultural studies to Prep to Year 7, and tutoring certificate III in teacher aide to an open adult class. That was a lot of teaching! To top it all off I continued freelancing at other schools teaching cultural awareness and contemporary Indigenous dance, particularly at private schools in the region. I was also performing on and off. But I began to sense that something was up with me physically. I tired almost immediately walking up stairs, would often feel drowsy driving to work in the morning, and would be almost nodding off at the wheel in the afternoons during the slow drive home. When I should've been quite fit, I was getting exhausted by the slightest things. I had no time for my house or my family, let alone myself.

This realisation had me concerned because I had planned to do a long walk from Aurukun, in the Western Cape, to Canberra early in 2009. This came about after being constantly bombarded with disturbing stories of the prevalence of child sexual abuse in Indigenous communities. This shocking business had disturbed me so profoundly that I wanted to do more than just be shocked. I wanted to quite literally walk out my utter contempt at such disgusting acts against our children. I wanted for my shock to be witnessed and heard by the nation.

I had begun speaking to various people and organisations about my intention to walk and had sent letters requesting support of any kind, whether it be financial, donation of resources or publicity. Many people offered their support or said they'd do a part of the walk with me as I passed through their respective towns or cities. My heart was deadset on it; there was no way I wasn't going to do this. I'd told the Murri School that I would be leaving at the end of 2008 to prepare, and that I would try to plan my route along Beaudesert Road so that the students could join me for however long the school was willing to allow them to participate.

But the walk did not eventuate as intended, well at least not at the time I had initially planned for it to anyway. By the end of 2008 I had been diagnosed with the return of ITP, which I had first developed back in 1991. My red blood cell count was dramatically low and apparently I was suffering, without me even really being aware of it, with depression. I'd known something was up, but had no idea my situation was this serious. Reluctantly, and severely disappointed, I had no choice but to postpone the walk indefinitely and focus on getting well again.

I was going to miss the Murri School. That place had been my substitute home. It was where I gathered with other Murris to cultivate our sense of collective belonging and identity in a society where we had been dispersed and pushed to the perimeters of society. Going there every day was like going *home* to Napranum for a visit in order to reconnect. Apart from my professional role at the Murri School, that's what it really meant to me. My spirit was happy in that school, regardless of the myriad challenges that presented themselves, constantly bombarding me. I especially loved the hugs from the kids, yarning with them and sitting on the grass sharing a feast with everyone on speech night or at other functions. I loved being surrounded by my people fully aware of the traffic that surrounded us and the buildings that towered in the distance, concrete spirits that now laid claim to this once untouched and beautiful land owned by the First Nations. The Murri School certainly satisfied my longing for a sense of home and identity in Brisbane, something I had been craving since our arrival back in 2004.

CHAPTER TWENTY-SEVEN

One afternoon after work I was sitting on the back veranda when the phone rang. It was Lyn.

'Fay, she hasn't got long to live.'

Yeah right, here we go again, I thought to myself. 'Lyn, how many times has she proved the doctors wrong and cheated death? Nan won't go until she's ready to.'

I remembered many a time watching Nan appear to stare death in the eye and fight to remain with us, each time with success. She would buck and bolt like a wild horse and rip tubes out from her nose or throat and proceed to jump off hospital beds. Nurses would really struggle to match Nan's physical strength and pin her down. Those white nurses were really no match for Nan, not even in her old age. That woman was strong in almost every aspect of her being!

'Yeah, I know Fay, but this time I reckon they're right. Nan does look tired. I think you should come up, like as soon as you can. Probably she's only got until the end of the week.'

Silence.

It's the weirdest thing being told that someone you love and that you've been loved by all your life will be departing the planet in a week or so. No matter how much you try to make sense of it, you will never ever quite grasp what it really means. It is the freakiest concept. 'Right, okay, I see. I'll make arrangements and let you know then.' And with that I hung up.

'Apparently she's going. Lyn wants me there as soon as,' I informed Dan.

'You probably won't recognise her, Fay,' Lyn said as we packed the bus with our luggage and headed straight for the hospital.

'What do you mean? Of course I'll recognise Nan.'

'She tired. She doesn't talk anymore, she just sleeps all the time now.'

I was quiet the rest of the way.

Some family members were in the room with Nan when we arrived. Most of them quickly left, allowing Sheridan and me time with her. Lyn was right. Who was this woman on the bed before me? She appeared to have already begun the journey of transition into the afterlife. Her heart may have still been ticking, but this was just a shell on the bed.

'Nan?' I whispered as I grabbed her hand.

Nothing.

'Nan, it's me, Fay, and I brought Nyrlotte with me. We came to see you.'

Nothing.

'Justice and Eb back in Brisbane with Danny.'

She squeezed my hand a little and attempted to say something. I couldn't recognise the words. It was all just slurred noises but it was obvious she was trying to respond.

I inwardly ached as my heart started to swell at the realisation that I was never going to hear my granny's voice again. The voice that had loved me, disciplined me, directed me, cared for me and taught me all my life was going to be no more. I placed my head on her chest, gently listening to her heartbeat.

We were fortunate to be able to remain at the hospital around the clock as Nan slowly prepared to depart. All the amenities were made available to us, providing of course that we did not interfere with the other patients. Nan was going to leave at any moment as her organs slowly began to shut down, one after the other. Mum had a bed near her while us others found places on the floor to sleep. Another room was made available for other members of the family. I was both surprised and extremely grateful that the Weipa Hospital accommodated us to such an extent, obviously taking cultural business into consideration. Although, if I'd had my way I would've taken Nan home or across the river back to country for her to make her exit. Regardless, the nurses and the system were cooperative and demonstrated appropriate respect.

On my first night I woke up in the middle of the night to see an older sister, who traditionally was really my aunty, sitting by Nan's bed holding her hand. Nan had cared for, loved and been there for Loyla from childhood and now here Loyla was to farewell Nan. Life is one long flow of circles, I thought. There's a start and a finish to everyone and everything at some point in time.

The next day I saw the nurses pottering around Nan.

'Uhm, excuse me, but what are you doing with her?'

'We need to move Gran to the bigger room.'

'Why?'

'She will leave today. Everything's shut down. The bigger room will fit families in.'

'How will we know?'

'Her breathing will indicate. There will be an obvious change in rhythm.'

Once Nan was comfortable again it was a matter of waiting. Families had started a game of Kun Kan in the back of the hospital. I existed somewhere between the bigger room Nan had been moved to and the circle of people playing Kun Kan.

Suddenly, late in the afternoon, my belly weighed down. I knew Nan was getting ready to go so I paid her a visit. I leaned against the wall and watched her, all the while paying special attention to her breathing. Suddenly her breathing changed both rhythm and pace; it was a lot slower. I rushed outside and indicated to Lyn that I thought – actually no – I *felt* it was time. As soon as Lyn got up, everyone else followed.

I looked at the clock. It was twenty to six.

The room slowly filled and was soon packed to the maximum. As if Nan was aware that everyone who could make her departure had arrived, her breathing rhythm changed yet again.

Two quick breaths in, and one long breath out.

Two quick breaths in, another long breath out.

The whole room was silent. Even the babies had stopped gooing and gahing and were watching her intently.

The last breath was two quick breaths in, and a long pause . . .

then one drawn-out slow, almost controlled breath out.

Never to take in another breath of oxygen again.

I looked up at the time. It was so my Nan, I thought to myself. Smack bang on six o'clock – her final performance.

She was always so pedantic about time.

Wow, I thought to myself. How deadly was that exit? There was no struggle, no gasping for air, no pain evident in her body, nothing. Her exit was smooth and controlled.

Silence for several more seconds and then the wailing began. I just stood there, looking at the shell that once housed the one woman who took care of me after my grandfather passed when I was ten. She just laid there. People were crying and wailing and talking, both in the room and out in the corridor. The hospital staff let us do our thing.

About thirty minutes later everyone had to leave the room while all Nan's little sisters, headed by Kathleen Vida, my younger sister, began to wash Nan down, dress her in her favourite dress and prepare her. Once she was ready they proceeded to take her out the back. The people now began to surround the morgue and continued to mourn for another hour or so. Lynette started complaining about the stretcher that would be used to carry her. I looked at it and understood why she didn't like this one. It was too thin and looked gammon, but I didn't have any strength to say anything.

I followed Nan to the morgue. I didn't like the look of the place and I didn't want to put Nan in there. It was cold and I knew she would be lonely. It sent shivers through me and only then did I begin to cry.

Once they'd zipped Nan into the bag I noticed some of her hair peeping out. I pointed it out to Lyn. Lyn let Bob know and he tucked it in. They shut the door. Families continued to sit outside the morgue mourning for several more hours.

'She's gone,' I told Dan later that night.

He didn't respond. It had been three days since Lyn suggested I fly up.

'Send the girls up asap.'

He did and then went bush to walk the line and earn some more money.

A couple of days before the funeral I felt that Danny should have been there to farewell Nan proper way. She had loved him like her own grandson, she would've wanted him to be there. The next time he called me I told him how I felt about him being at the farewell. He made preparations to attend and made it just in time.

On the day of the funeral, 1 Peppan Street was surrounded by cars and people both inside the yard and all around it. We had requested that everyone dress in orange, one of Nan's favourite colours. There was white sand at the back with a table placed right in the middle of it. This was where Nan would rest for the last time before being taken up to the church. Everyone waited quietly. The dancers were somewhere in hiding, waiting to welcome the body through ceremony as is custom. The waiting lasted several hours and I began to wonder why there was such a long delay.

We later found out that the men went to the hospital morgue without the coffin and had to drive all the way back to Naps to get it. Then something else went wrong, delaying her arrival even more. It was the longest wait.

Afterwards Dan told me that he had initially felt nothing as they placed Nan into the back of the hearse with him. Yet, once they got to Ewrpwin he felt her presence strong. As they approached the turn off into Napranum apparently a big gust of wind came up past the car and continued down the road. Right at that point I felt the wind travel down the road and saw it upturn the tarpaulin and knock over the palm trees that surrounded the table. I immediately stood up. I knew from the arrival of *mboormbwin* that Nan wasn't far away. Again, I indicated to Lyn and like clockwork everyone else stood to their feet to await her arrival.

The ceremony of song and dance began as the hearse pulled up at the front. I looked around to see where Mum was. I spotted her sitting in the front row of seats, just opposite to where the coffin would be placed. She appeared devoid of emotion. There was no crying or wailing on her part. I wondered what she was feeling. This was her mother arriving. That strong, tall, outspoken woman who carried our family for the past eighty years or so had arrived to spend her final hour at 1 Peppan Street.

Apalich and Wikway welcomed her to the house for the final time.

Lyn and I had decided to have Nan's room opening as soon as possible as opposed to having a drawn-out wait of one to two years. Lyn wanted to use the room Nan had occupied during her stay at the Peppan Street house for the ceremony. Usually the whole house would be locked up but because Lyn decided to continue to occupy the house she opted to break custom and limited closure to just one room. Mum understood the situation and gave us the go-ahead. Nan passed away in July and we decided to have the room opening almost immediately in October. Besides, *Chitch* Silas, Nan's brother, hadn't been eating big meat since Nan's passing and was fast losing weight. This was dangerous for an elder of his age, as it could affect his health. But he had made it quite clear to us that he wasn't going to break protocol when it came to his big sister; he was not allowed to consume any type of big or fat meat until follow-up ceremony was done, to once and for all send Nan's spirit back to country and her final resting place. So doing it more quickly was for his sake as well. Dan, the girls and I flew to Cairns and then booked a hire car and drove to Weipa. A bus was arranged to transport families from Aurukun, particularly the singers and dancers along with their respective families.

My three girls, along with their cousins, were required to participate in activities that were part of the lead-up to the actual opening ceremony. They intently followed *Chitch* Silas's wife, Granny Rebecca Wolmby, around, observing every step and preparation she demonstrated to them. Lyn's house had been decorated all around the outside with palm leaves, balloons and crepe paper. At the front entrance was an arrangement of dilly bags, fruit baskets, mats, feather flowers and so on.

Sheridan, Justice and Ebony were required to participate in the painting up of all the widows with charcoal and then wash them down, which was symbolic of the recognition of one phase ending and a new one beginning. The widows are all those that have married into Nan's maternal nation – male or female – to any member that is of Nan's generation. As a result of Nan's passing, all those in-laws who are left behind are now considered widowed. These widows must be washed down by the younger generations of our bloodline to symbolise the passing. This ceremony repeated itself just as I had experienced it as a child when my grandad passed. My children witnessed what I had back in the seventies.

Immediately following the funeral, family members who could weave got started on the artefacts specifically required for this opening ceremony. People were forbidden from touching these artefacts until it was indicated they could do so. Sheridan had been selected to cut the ribbon so people could enter the house, and particularly Nan's room, to begin the second mourning stage. As people entered the room, mourned her spirit and left, more people were allowed in to do the same until such time as everyone who had desired to farewell her spirit in this way had the chance to.

The chopping of Nan's name was next and this time Ebony, who also carries the name Awumpan, was invited to the centre where this particular part of the ceremony was to be carried out. Each name Nan was known by – Jean . . . Awumpun . . . George – was said followed an axe chopping into the wood twice after each word had been spoken. This now meant that her name could be spoken freely. The substitute name to refer to a deceased person is *tharpitch*. Prior to this it would've been breaking protocol to have said her name under any circumstances, although there are a few exceptions such as during the service at the funeral.

Meanwhile, out the front of the house, families had begun the dancing and singing component of the ceremony, as those lucky enough to get to the traditional artefacts on display made claim to whatever it was they wanted.

I ate wild geese just before we were to drive back to Cairns that evening and, because I love this wild game and grew up on it as a child, foolishly I ate more than I should have. Several hours into the drive I could not hold any of the meat down. Had I become so urbanised that I couldn't even handle traditional food anymore?

Leaving Weipa behind following Nan's house opening was like saying goodbye once and for all. This land was, and still is, the land of my forefathers, this land was where my feet ran wild as a child, everything about it contributed to me cultivating a sense of my own identity – the smell of it, the way the heat sits on my skin, the way *oolay waarth* calls out in the middle of the day, the way the earth feels after rain has danced with it. Now that Nan was gone, it was time for me to move on to the next phase of my life, whatever that entailed.

POSTSCRIPT

Early in 2008, not long after the preview season of *Whispers of This Wik Woman*, the theatre adaptation of Nan's story, Danny and I divorced. We had clocked up eighteen years of marriage.

Just over a year later, in February 2009, I moved to Cairns to take up a position as coordinator of the Performing Arts Programme, which was supported by Education Queensland's Indigenous Schooling Support Unit. I absolutely loved my brief time working with young people from the Cape and exploring contemporary Indigenous movement once more. It reminded me of the role Lillian Crombie and Aunty Sylvia Blanco played back in the eighties in setting an example for me and urging me to aspire to a career in dance. Here I was, several decades later, repeating the process – and this time I was in the driver's seat. I was thrilled when several of the youngsters successfully auditioned for Naisda. It seemed the vital cycle of support and role-modelling was continuing.

I also visited country that year with Natjul Indigenous Performing Arts company using forum theatre – a style of theatre we used to address the social issues impacting the Cape communities. To be a part of a team once more with Anthony, Tom and Steve – the team I worked with on *Yesterday Now* back in 2004 – as well as Brother Matty Collins, who joined us as a counsellor, and see families engage in dialogue was very satisfying. This type of approach strikes me as having the potential to play an important role in instigating change for the better for my people. I would love to see this work continue, not only across the Cape York region but across the nation as a whole. Identity is so crucial to our sense of self; it is central to our very existence. Our spirits are fat and content when our sense of who we are is full and complete and dance, dramatic re-enactment, stories, songs, art and kinship systems are all part and parcel of that.

Late in 2009, the girls and I returned to Brisbane. By that point I had come to a standstill. Something had shifted in me and suddenly things did not seem so sweet. I began to sink in every way. Indeed, 2010 was the most challenging year of my whole life. It seemed that everything had fallen apart. For the first time I realised my family was no longer the strong, tight unit it once was. My husband was gone; in fact, on paper he was no longer my husband, yet no part of me could accept that. I could not see myself living the rest of my life without Danny in it, without the girls and us being the family that we once were. Back in 1990, he and I had made a promise to each other and then had created these beautiful girls, and now it was over. I did not understand what happened.

Where had we gone wrong? The couple of years leading up to the divorce had been one big blur. Now I just wanted my family back together again, but it appeared this was not meant to be.

Writing was my constant companion through those bleak times. *Jindah Murray: Wind Dancer*, a children's book, was published by Oxford University Press early in 2011. At the same time I was writing that I was working on this memoir. I lived in my cave and kept almost everyone out. Each time I looked in the mirror I did not recognise the woman staring back at me. I cannot even begin to describe the sense of hopelessness and despair that gripped me.

Towards the tail end of 2010 I knew that it was time to make a decision. I could either sink or swim. I had been in pain long enough. I found the strength to live by simply looking at the faces of my beautiful daughters Sheridan, Justice and Ebony. I decided to return to study. I enrolled in a Master of Education with a focus on school guidance and counselling. The course keeps me both busy and focused. I have also re-established a strong sense of faith in my God. I have learnt to simply say no if and when I need to. Although, the upshot of my priorities having changed so immensely is that some professional projects that I had intended to pursue over the next couple of years have been shelved indefinitely. One is *Soul Yarn*, a multimedia presentation using dance, theatre and live music, and another is *Blak Velvet*, a theatre piece.

Another project that has been put on hold is my walk from Napranum to Canberra to raise awareness about the prevalence of child sexual abuse in Indigenous communities, which twice before (in 2009 and 2010) has been cancelled. Only time will tell if the opportunity to go ahead will present itself.

Occasionally I give a talk or presentation about my work and achievements to date or run a dance workshop, but my life now is more about balance and prioritising things that are healthy and productive for both myself and my daughters. The girls are growing so incredibly fast. Sheridan is now nineteen and has left home, Justice is sixteen and Ebony is twelve. I still miss my family as we once were beyond words.

I maintain contact with my Austrian relatives, mainly through Ulrike. The family has sent word that they are looking forward to the release of *Double Native*. One day I would like to return to Salzburg with Sheridan, Justice and Ebony. It is important for them to see and experience their grandfather's history for themselves. His identity is part of theirs. I believe the opportunity will present itself in its season.

Right now I don't quite know where I am headed. Even though an uncertain future at one stage conjured up intense fear beyond words I realise now that I'm doing alright. My life is in the hands of someone who is greater. I am now focusing on my daughters and on just being. I have learnt more than a handful of valuable lessons in recent years, all of them the hard way. I did indeed dance with darkness. These days, however, I am stronger and more settled. My spirit and mind are steady. Who knows what *mboormbwin* has in store for me. I will just have to walk the rest of my journey out for as long as I am allowed to breathe.